REUNION REVIVAL

Rediscovering Faith, Family, and Community with Jesus

REUNION REVIVAL

Rediscovering Faith, Family, and Community with Jesus

Compiled and edited
by Cheryl L. Price, Ph.D.

Urban Ministries, Inc.

Urban Ministries, Inc.

UMI (Urban Ministries, Inc.)
P.O. Box 436987
Chicago, Illinois 60643-6987

www.urbanministries.com

First Edition
First Printing

Scripture quotations marked KJV, or unmarked, are from the King James Version.

Scripture quotations marked NIV are taken from the HOLY BIBLE, NEW INTERNATIONAL VERSION®, copyright© 1973, 1978, 1984 Biblica. Used by permission of Zondervan. All rights reserved.

Scripture quotations marked NLT are taken from the Holy Bible, New Living Translation, copyright© 1996, 2004. Used by permission of Tyndale House Publishers, Inc., Wheaton, Illinois 60189. All rights reserved.

Scripture quotations marked NASB are taken from the NEW AMERICAN STANDARD BIBLE®, copyright© 1960, 1962, 1963, 1968, 1971, 1972, 1973, 1975, 1977, 1995 by The Lockman Foundation. Used by permission.

Reunion Revival: Rediscovering Faith, Family, and Community with Jesus has been compiled and edited by Cheryl L. Price, Ph.D.

Library of Congress Cataloging in Publications Data

ISBN-10: 1-60997-620-7

ISBN-13: 978-1-60997-620-0

1. Christian living   2. African American

Library of Congress Control Number: 2013933501

Printed in the United States of America.

DEDICATION

Reunion Revival: Rediscovering Faith, Family, and Community with Jesus is dedicated to all Christian Education teachers and students.

Table of Contents

* Recommended for five-day Bible curriculum

Reunion Revival

REDISCOVERING FAITH, FAMILY, AND COMMUNITY WITH JESUS

Stop! Think about the first time you discovered Jesus for yourself and accepted Him into your life. What a joyous, refreshing, and freeing moment! There are times when our lives become so busy or so burdened that we need to stop and revisit the first time we accepted Jesus as our personal Savior. By rediscovering that time and reflecting on how we have since broadened and deepened our understanding of Christ, we can revive our faith walk with Christ. In doing so, we enhance our relationships with our families and our communities to become more inclusive of others. Therefore, it's time to have a "Reunion Revival" to rediscover our faith, family, and community with Jesus.

When we revive our relationship with Christ, we may have to shift our thinking from "business as usual" to more dynamic—and possibly uncomfortable—ways of being like Christ. For example, when you hear or read the word "family," what images come to mind? Do you think of the traditional image of family as a father, mother, and children? Do you imagine a mother or a father and a child? Perhaps you think of grandparents or great-grandparents surrounded by multiple generations of children that may include nieces, nephews, and cousins. Maybe you think of a young person whose close friends have become his or her self-selected "family." Remember, our various notions of "family" represent the glue that holds society accountable to the joys and needs of our respective communities and society overall.

Yet our faith, family, and community have come under attack spiritually, socially, physically, and psychologically. Particularly in the African American community, the chaotic and disruptive issues that plague our families have kept us in destructive holding patterns internally and externally. The number of incarcerated African American males and females has increased over the years along with the number of HIV/AIDS cases, the number of parents leaving their families to go to war, mental health issues, the unemployment rate, the increase of female-headed households, and additional social needs and crises have had—and continue to have—an impact on the African American family. These issues—and more—affect our faith, our worship of Christ, our ability to communicate with one another, and so much more.

Although our "family picture" looks grim and hopeless at times, God has not left us without the faith, creativity, skills, passion, and tenacity to make changes. Redefining the family and enhancing current family relationships are necessary to cultivate healthier and stronger units within our community. Our faith and the role of the church are keys to the spiritual development and well-being of African American families. Families need to learn, worship, and serve God in unison. As Joshua said, "As for me and my house, we will serve the LORD" (Joshua 24:15, KJV).

As you study *Reunion Revival: Rediscovering Faith, Family, and Community with Jesus*, you will experience lessons that teach and encourage families to worship and deepen their knowledge of God's Word. "Faith, family, and community" are expressed in the book's ten chapters to include those who are related by blood as well as those who become a family because of the love and support they show each other. Paul and Timothy, in Chapter 1, are examples of this type of family; Paul was not related to Timothy, but he became like a father to Timothy.

The ten chapters of *Reunion Revival* that connect faith, family, and community are:

1. Faith: Believe or Not!
2. Standing in the Gap
3. Forgiveness? Why?
4. Protecting Family
5. My Jars Are Empty
6. The Gift of Love
7. It Is Amazing!
8. A Family Affair
9. Astonishing Growth!
10. God Gives Us a Fresh Start

As you read and study *Reunion Revival: Rediscovering Faith, Family, and Community with Jesus,* we know you will find the lessons a treasure of information that will increase your biblical understanding and allow you and your family to study God's Word as one. Why not invite your family and your extended family to study with you? The more "family members" in concert with studying God's Word, the more opportunities to share the Word with others and learn from one another become available.

1

Faith: Believe or Not!

LESSON SCRIPTURE
2 TIMOTHY 1:2–10, 13–14

BACKGROUND SCRIPTURES
2 Timothy 1:1-14; Acts 11:23-24; John 4:24; Acts 16:2; 1 Timothy 4:12

QUESTION
Separation from loved ones—for whatever reason—can be difficult. Think of a time when you, as a parent or a child, were separated from a loved one. What created the connection you had with that person? What was your greatest desire during that separation?

SEPARATED BY TIME AND SPACE
Although Shelli was the older sister, she felt she had been the mother figure in her younger brothers' lives. After their parents died in a crash, Shelli—then just 20 years old—stepped up to care for her 10-year-old twin brothers. She tried to instill in them everything their parents had given her. She kept them active in church, sports, and community activities, always with a mind toward college. They had done well. They'd given her no problems but now that the twins attended schools in separate states, she realized that all their lives would be changed forever.

When she dropped the twins off at their respective campuses, she realized that their choices would now be their own. No more monitoring their activities. In her heart, she knew she'd done everything her parents would have done. As she drove home, the loneliness hit her and she began to cry. Then she whispered a prayer: "Lord, keep them safe and help them remember who You are in their lives."

DISCUSSION
How would you describe Shelli's anxiety over her brothers' well-being? Why do you think it is so difficult for her to let go? What role do you think her faith and her brothers' faith will play in their future?

TRANSITION
Paul wrote to Timothy and reminded him of the faith that was instilled in him as a child by his mother and grandmother. In addition, Paul's tone shows his own love and care for Timothy as his dear son in the Lord (1 Timothy 1:2). Although Timothy was a pastor, Paul felt the need to remind him of the legacy of faith he had been given and the message of faith he was to uphold and preach. Similarly, Shelli feels the tension of letting her brothers go, knowing she has given them all she could in terms of their upbringing in the faith and praying that they will be ever-mindful of God in their lives. This passage reminds us that faith is critical to developing a strong relationship with God and that we have an obligation to pass the faith to the next generation.

SCRIPTURE VOCABULARY
Forefathers (v. 3) — Paul's reference is to the fathers of the faith (Abraham, Isaac, and Jacob).

Unfeigned (v. 5) — Sincere

Stir up (v. 6) — This is translated as "fan the flames" (NIV) or "keep ablaze." It can be considered the active pursuit of the gift and ministry God gives us.

SCRIPTURE REFERENCE

2 TIMOTHY 1:2–10, 13–14

2 To Timothy, my dearly beloved son: Grace, mercy, and peace, from God the Father and Christ Jesus our Lord.

3 I thank God, whom I serve from my forefathers with pure conscience, that without ceasing I have remembrance of thee in my prayers night and day;

4 Greatly desiring to see thee, being mindful of thy tears, that I may be filled with joy;

5 When I call to remembrance the unfeigned faith that is in thee, which dwelt first in thy grandmother Lois, and thy mother Eunice; and I am persuaded that in thee also.

6 Wherefore I put thee in remembrance that thou stir up the gift of God, which is in thee by the putting on of my hands.

7 For God hath not given us the spirit of fear; but of power, and of love, and of a sound mind.

8 Be not thou therefore ashamed of the testimony of our Lord, nor of me his prisoner: but be thou partaker of the afflictions of the gospel according to the power of God;

9 Who hath saved us, and called us with an holy calling, not according to our works, but according to his own purpose and grace, which was given us in Christ Jesus before the world began,

10 But is now made manifest by the appearing of our Saviour Jesus Christ, who hath abolished death, and hath brought life and immortality to light through the gospel:

1:13 Hold fast the form of sound words, which thou hast heard of me, in faith and love which is in Christ Jesus.

14 That good thing which was committed unto thee keep by the Holy Ghost which dwelleth in us.

MEMORY VERSE

"Whosoever believeth on him shall not be ashamed" (from Romans 9:33, KJV).

HOW DOES THE MEMORY VERSE APPLY TO YOUR FAITH WALK?

_____

_____

LESSON FOCUS
Believing in God collectively builds a family legacy. Paul reminds Timothy of the legacy of faith his family has given him as well as the faith he has declared, according to the gifts God has placed in his life. As witnesses of Jesus Christ, each of us should be mindful that we are strengthened when we remind one another of what God has done and is calling us to do in our lives. With that resolve, we are able to share the Gospel message without fear or shame.

BIBLE BACKGROUND
Paul writes this second and final letter to Timothy, who is pastoring the church in Ephesus. This letter was written in 66 A.D., about four years after First Timothy. Paul, who had been placed on trial for declaring the Gospel of Jesus Christ, was facing a death sentence he knew would be soon carried out. Previously, he had been placed under house arrest in Rome but was allowed to have visitors. This is a subsequent imprisonment and Paul was likely held in a dungeon. Despite his chains and isolation, he continued to share the Gospel, particularly by encouraging the churches he helped to establish. At this point, only Luke has remained with him, and the loneliness of his situation is heard in the tone of the letter. Nevertheless, Paul reminds Timothy of what the young preacher learned from him and from his mother and grandmother regarding faith in Jesus Christ. Paul encourages Timothy to be strong and bold

in his ministry, knowing that no matter what persecution he faced, he must never be ashamed of or turn his back on the Gospel of Jesus Christ.

SCRIPTURE EXPLORATION

> *2 Timothy 1:2-6—To Timothy, my dearly beloved son: Grace, mercy, and peace, from God the Father and Christ Jesus our Lord. 3 I thank God, whom I serve from my forefathers with pure conscience, that without ceasing I have remembrance of thee in my prayers night and day; 4 Greatly desiring to see thee, being mindful of thy tears, that I may be filled with joy; 5 When I call to remembrance the unfeigned faith that is in thee, which dwelt first in thy grandmother Lois, and thy mother Eunice; and I am persuaded that in thee also. 6 Wherefore I put thee in remembrance that thou stir up the gift of God, which is in thee by the putting on of my hands.*

Paul's trial in Rome was not the only persecution he had faced. He had been called to explain and justify his claim of Jewish heritage many times. Paul saw his faith in Jesus Christ as the fulfillment of all it meant to be a Jew. He did not renounce his Jewishness; rather, he rejoiced that as a Jew, he realized the fulfillment of prophecy regarding the coming Messiah and the work of God in the world. To this end, his letters explained the Gospel in terms of the history and prophecies of the Torah. But Paul also recognized that the Word was not only to the Jew. Rather, it was to the Jew first and then to the Greek (Romans 1:16). Because of that, Paul was able to share his faith "with good conscience" and to pray for all who accepted and proclaimed the Gospel of Jesus Christ, regardless of his or her national origin.

There is no doubt Paul loved Timothy. In verse 3, he declares that he prays for this young son in the Lord both "night and day." Furthermore, Paul longed to see Timothy again and knew that Timothy was distressed over his imprisonment and pending death. The two had become close during Paul's second and third missionary journeys, when young Timothy traveled as Paul's protégé. Paul also lets Timothy know that seeing him would both stop Timothy's tears and bring Paul joy. Unfortunately, their meeting was never to take place.

Paul not only knew Timothy, he knew Timothy's family as well. Timothy's father was a Roman soldier and his mother was a Jewish believer. It is through his grandmother, Lois, and mother, Eunice, that Timothy was introduced to the Gospel of Jesus Christ and saved to the glory of God. These women had a sincere faith, meaning they were authentic and bold in their witness for Jesus Christ. This is the boldness they passed to their son. Timothy was rooted and grounded in the sacred Scriptures and had an understanding of the work of Jesus in his life and the lives of those around him. This is the faith Paul saw in Lois and Eunice and knew was in Timothy.

Perhaps that is why Paul took Timothy, despite his youth, with him on his missionary journeys. Paul reminds Timothy that he was called into ministry—into a work that provided the avenue through which he would proclaim the Gospel— when Paul prayed for him and laid hands on him. This does not mean that Paul gave Timothy some spiritual gift or even that Paul asked God to give Timothy a gift. It means that Paul confirmed, through public prayer and declaration, the gift that was obviously placed in Timothy's life by the Holy Spirit. In other words, Paul is reminding Timothy of his upbringing as a third-generation believer (even though

Christianity was relatively new) and his ordination as a minister of the Gospel.

v. 7 — For God hath not given us the spirit of fear; but of power, and of love, and of a sound mind.

Paul writes Timothy to encourage him. By this time, the persecution of the church was brutal. The Emperor Nero had placed blame for the great fire of Rome on Christians—even though he set the fire himself! The result was public torture, public executions, and terrorism as Christians were unmercifully hunted. Many Christians were turning back, denouncing Jesus to save their lives and the lives of their loved ones. Even before persecution became so profound, teaching that was contrary to the truth of the Gospel had started to pervert the message of the Gospel, and it was necessary that those who knew the truth proclaim it boldly and without compromise. It is no wonder then that Paul felt the need to encourage Timothy to be faithful to the Gospel and to his ministry as a pastor and teacher.

In these verses, Paul also reminds Timothy that God has not given him the spirit of fear (Gk. *deilia*, timidity)! Regardless of the slaughtering, persecution, and hunting of Christians by those who sought favor from the emperor, fear or dread were not to take hold of the believer and force him or her to turn away from the truth. Paul understood that apprehension and concern were natural, given the times, but his declaration is that such a controlling "spirit" (Gk. *pneuma*) was not from God. Even in the midst of turmoil and trial, God gives believers power (Gk. *dunamis*), love (Gk. *agape*), and a sound mind (Gk. *sophronismos*, disciple and self-control). In other words, regardless of what we face, God has provided, through His Spirit, the dynamic power to sacrificially love others and exercise the self-control and discipline to continue to lift up

Jesus without faltering in the faith. That is a tall order, and it is why Paul felt it so urgent to encourage Timothy.

> *vv. 8–10 — Be not thou therefore ashamed of the testimony of our Lord, nor of me his prisoner: but be thou partaker of the afflictions of the gospel according to the power of God; 9 Who hath saved us, and called us with an holy calling, not according to our works, but according to his own purpose and grace, which was given us in Christ Jesus before the world began, 10 But is now made manifest by the appearing of our Saviour Jesus Christ, who hath abolished death, and hath brought life and immortality to light through the gospel:*

Given God's provision of power, love, and self-control, Paul tells Timothy not to be ashamed of either the Gospel or his own state of bondage and pending death. Paul does not, however, stop there. He encourages Timothy to endure the affliction that is sure to come to him and to those in his church. This was real, and both Paul and Timothy knew it. Paul's rationale for how Timothy was to endure, however, was equally powerful. Timothy was to hold on because of the power of God. God's power was sufficient for the persecution that would come. His power would not wane or abate. It would not give in to the pressure of the Roman Empire. It was the depth and strength of God's power that saved Paul from his disbelief, nurtured Timothy's faith, and called them into the noble and holy work of the ministry. Timothy is told he would not endure according to his own power or reputation as a preacher and teacher, nor would he endure because he was doing a good work that was respected in the community. He would endure only because it was God's express and public purpose (Gk. *prothesis*) for him to endure. He would endure because God selected him, gave him the favor (Gk. *charis*, grace) to endure. This was not a recent development or idea in God's mind. This purpose and grace was given by God in Jesus Christ before the world even began. There is nothing that can overtake the believer that God does not know. Nothing can overtake the believer because God has already given us the power to endure! This is no ordinary power. This is the power Jesus Christ exercised in abolishing death. It is the power the Gospel contains that gives life and immortality to those who believe.

vv. 13–14 — Hold fast the form of sound words, which thou hast heard of me, in faith and love which is in Christ Jesus. 14 That good thing which was committed unto thee keep by the Holy Ghost which dwelleth in us.

In these two verses, Paul sums up his message of encouragement. The New Living Translation puts it this way: "Hold on to the pattern of wholesome teaching you learned from me—a pattern shaped by the faith and love that you have in Christ Jesus." Furthermore, Paul adds, "Through the power of the Holy Spirit who lives within us, carefully guard the precious truth that has been entrusted to you."

DISCUSSION
1. What does Paul's letter teach us about the necessity of maintaining the fellowship of believers?
2. What encouragement does this Scripture text give parents and mentors in the church? Does Paul consider these relationships and teachings optional? Why or why not?
3. Do we have the option to believe in isolation, living without fellowship and without sharing the Gospel message with others?
4. Women did not have a place of prominence in Jewish

circles, nor were women considered equal to men during this time period. Why did Paul choose to highlight the faith of Lois and Eunice?

5. What implications does Paul's statement about the "laying on of hands" have for the church today?

6. Why does Paul choose to highlight rather than downplay his own plight and pending death?

PRACTICAL APPLICATION
PERSONAL APPLICATION

1. We could glibly say we would never be ashamed of the Gospel, but if we reflect, we will realize there have been times when we were less than forthright in sharing the Gospel message with others. Create a list of situations when Christians might be reticent to witness or defend our faith. What role does race, denomination, class, power, or insecurity play in our decisions? Compare your list with someone else's.

2. Paul constantly calls on Timothy to "remember." Identify those people who taught you, nurtured you, or witnessed to you about being a Christian. Consider how they did their work. Was this with words only? Did they exhibit an "unfeigned" or sincere faith? How? How have you adopted their teachings into your life? How have you passed the faith to others in your family or community?

COMMUNITY APPLICATION

1. We live in a time when shame reigns. We are ashamed of our communities and of those who do not exemplify the values we hold as Christians. Perhaps the question should be

asked: "What have we done to share the values our African American and Christian forefathers held so dear?" Gather the seniors, children, youth, and peers in your family or community and discuss how to "pass it on." Consider:

- What attitudes have developed in your family and community toward those who are unsaved or who seem to have forgotten the struggles of Black people to gain respect from all segments of society?

- What effort should members of your family and community make to encourage less violence, more respect, and greater civility? What hinders family and community members from sharing this encouragement with others? What role does fear play when we choose to share or not share these truths? How would Paul encourage us?

2. Paul's letter was written to Timothy, a pastor. It is obvious the letter was addressed to churches—even those in our day—and not just to a single pastor. This begs the question of how the church is maintaining Paul's message of strength in the face of turmoil, incivility, and violence. Is the church doing enough today to turn our communities around? Why or why not? Develop a plan you can take to your church's pastor or auxiliary staff that includes ideas on: (a) how to encourage members of the congregation to be strong in their faith, and (b) how to help the community take advantage of the strength and hope Jesus Christ offers for our lives.

MEDITATION
Encourage my soul, Lord, to reflect on who You are in my life and in the lives of others. Encourage me to have quiet

moments to remind myself of Your love, support, and patience. Encourage my mind to know You as the One I can depend on each and every day. Thank You for encouraging the people in my life who guide me in the right direction and make time to be there for me. We all need encouragement to make it through life's journey.

PRAYER

Oh God, renew in us the desire to share who You are with others. Allow our faith in You to serve as a witness to others that You are faithful and steadfast. Keep us in Your care as we embrace, support, and give of ourselves to those who need to know more of who You are and who we are in You. In the name of Jesus we pray, amen.

BIBLIOGRAPHY

Life Application Study Bible—NIV. Wheaton, IL: Tyndale House, 1991. 2197-2199.

Strong, James. *Strong's Exhaustive Concordance*. Grand Rapids, MI: Baker Book House, 1977.

2

Standing in the Gap

LESSON SCRIPTURE
EXODUS 18:1, 9, 13-24

BACKGROUND SCRIPTURES
Exodus 2:18; 18; 2 Corinthians 13:11; 1 Thessalonians 4:18; 1
Timothy 5:1; Titus 2:2, 6; Hebrews 10:25

QUESTION
Describe an experience when someone encouraged you to
make a decision that made your life better.

REV. JONES WANTS TO BE INVOLVED
Rev. Jones was a young preacher who was recently assigned
to pastor his first church. He was excited about the prospect of
leading God's people. During the first few months, Rev. Jones
attended every meeting each ministry group held. He refused
to delegate any assignments to his assistants, Rev. Smith and
Rev. Jackson. Additionally, Rev. Jones consistently allowed
people to bypass his secretary and meet with him without an
appointment.

A few months into his tenure, Rev. Sullivan, the district
superintendent, visited Rev. Jones to assess his progress at
the church. During the meeting, several members of the
congregation knocked on the office door to speak with Rev.
Jones. After the third interruption, Rev. Sullivan understood the
bad habits Rev. Jones had developed. Rev. Sullivan cautioned
Rev. Jones to delegate responsibility to his assistants so they

could attend meetings with the various ministries and then report to Rev. Jones. Moreover, Rev. Sullivan stressed the importance of using his secretary to screen messages and appointments. Rev. Jones' current behavior was unsustainable. Although he was initially reluctant to change, Rev. Jones did heed the warnings.

DISCUSSION
Why do you think Rev. Jones wanted to be so deeply involved with the members and ministries of the church?

TRANSITION
Our story demonstrates the importance of a seasoned person guiding an inexperienced individual.

SCRIPTURE VOCABULARY
Counsel – Advice, recommendation
Judge – A person who hears disputes and decides the outcome.
Statutes – Laws, rules
Hearken – To listen, hear, or give heed to someone, usually someone who is giving advice.

SCRIPTURE REFERENCE
EXODUS 18:1, 9, 13-24

18:1 When Jethro, the priest of Midian, Moses' father-in-law, heard of all that God had done for Moses, and for Israel his people, and that the LORD had brought Israel out of Egypt;

18:9 And Jethro rejoiced for all the goodness which the LORD had done to Israel, whom he had delivered out of the hand of the Egyptians.

18:13 And it came to pass on the morrow, that Moses sat to judge the people: and the people stood by Moses from the morning unto the evening.

14 And when Moses' father in law saw all that he did to the people, he said, What is this thing that thou doest to the people? why sittest thou thyself alone, and all the people stand by thee from morning unto even?

15 And Moses said unto his father in law, Because the people come unto me to enquire of God:

16 When they have a matter, they come unto me; and I judge between one and another, and I do make them know the statutes of God, and his laws.

17 And Moses' father-in-law said unto him, The thing that thou doest is not good.

18 Thou wilt surely wear away, both thou, and this people that is with thee: for this thing is too heavy for thee; thou art not able to perform it thyself alone.

19 Hearken now unto my voice, I will give thee counsel, and God shall be with thee: Be thou for the people to God-ward, that thou mayest bring the causes unto God:

20 And thou shalt teach them ordinances and laws, and shalt shew them the way wherein they must walk, and the work that they must do.

21 Moreover thou shalt provide out of all the people able men, such as fear God, men of truth, hating covetousness; and place such over them, to be rulers of thousands, and rulers of hundreds, rulers of fifties, and rulers of tens:

22 And let them judge the people at all seasons: and it shall be, that every great matter they shall bring unto thee, but every small matter they shall judge: so shall it be easier for thyself, and they shall bear the burden with thee.

23 If thou shalt do this thing, and God command thee so, then thou shalt be able to endure, and all this people shall also go to their place in peace.

24 So Moses hearkened to the voice of his father-in-law, and did all that he had said.

MEMORY VERSE
"Exhort one another daily, while it is called To day"
(from Hebrews 3:13).

HOW DOES THE MEMORY VERSE APPLY TO YOUR FAITH WALK?

_____

_____

LESSON FOCUS
Jethro recognized that Moses' method of judging the people of Israel would take too much time and energy for Moses to do by himself. Jethro gave Moses advice on how to choose judges and delegate authority to them. Moses was obedient to Jethro's advice and appointed judges to hear the disputes of the people of Israel.

BIBLE BACKGROUND
Moses rescued the people of Israel from slavery in Egypt. As Moses and the people traveled in the wilderness for 40 years, Moses presided over disputes and controversies among the people. Jethro, Moses' father-in-law, originated from the land of Midian. Jethro decided to visit Moses in the wilderness after Jethro heard about the deliverance of the Israelites from Egypt.

SCRIPTURE EXPLORATION

Exodus 18:1-6—18 When Jethro, the priest of Midian, Moses' father in law, heard of all that God had done for Moses, and for Israel his people, and that the LORD had brought Israel out of Egypt; 2 Then Jethro, Moses' father in law, took Zipporah, Moses' wife, after he had sent her back, 3 And her two sons; of which the name of the one was Gershom; for he said, I have been an alien in a strange land: 4 And the name of the other was Eliezer; for the God of my father, said he, was mine help, and delivered me from the sword of Pharaoh: 5 And Jethro, Moses' father-in-law, came with his sons and his wife unto Moses into the wilderness, where he encamped at the mount of God: 6 And he said unto Moses, I thy father-in-law Jethro am come unto thee, and thy wife, and her two sons with her.

Moses married Jethro's daughter, Zipporah, during the 40 years he spent in Midian. For his safety, Moses had to flee from Egypt after he killed an Egyptian (Exodus 2:11-15). During their marriage, Zipporah gave birth to Gershom and Eliezer. Moses' family joined him when he returned to Egypt to deliver his people from bondage. At one point, however, Moses sent Zipporah and their two sons back to Midian to live with Jethro. When Jethro heard all that God had done in delivering Moses and the tribes of Israel from slavery in Egypt, Jethro brought Zipporah and their two sons back to Moses.

Exodus 18:8-10—And Moses told his father-in-law all that the LORD had done unto Pharaoh and to the Egyptians for Israel's sake, and all the travail that had come upon them by the way, and how the LORD delivered them. 9 And Jethro rejoiced for all the goodness which the LORD had done to Israel, whom he had delivered out of the hand of the Egyptians. 10 And Jethro said, Blessed be the LORD, who hath delivered you out of the hand of the Egyptians, and out of the hand of Pharaoh, who hath delivered the people from under the hand of the Egyptians.

When God delivered the people of Israel from bondage in Egypt, word of God's favor spread far and wide. Jethro celebrated the Israelites' victory over Pharaoh and the Egyptians. Although Jethro was not a member of the 12 tribes, he recognized God's power and authority. Jethro's statement in verse 10 underscores the meaning of the name Moses selected for Eliezer.

Exodus 18:13-24—And it came to pass on the morrow, that Moses sat to judge the people: and the people stood by Moses from the morning unto the evening. 14 And when Moses' father-in-law saw all that he did to the people, he said, What is this thing that thou doest to the people? why sittest thou thyself alone, and all the people stand by thee from morning unto even? 15 And Moses said unto his father-in-law, Because the people come unto me to enquire of God: 16 When they have a matter, they come unto me; and I judge between one and another, and I do make them know the statutes of God, and his laws. 17 And Moses' father-in-law said unto him, The thing that thou doest is not good. 18 Thou wilt surely wear away, both thou, and this people that is with thee: for this thing is too heavy for thee; thou art not able to perform it thyself alone. 19 Hearken now unto my voice, I will give thee counsel, and God shall be with thee: Be thou for the people to God-ward, that thou mayest bring the causes unto God: 20 And thou shalt teach them ordinances and laws, and shalt shew them the way wherein they must walk, and the work that they must do. 21 Moreover thou shalt provide out of all the people able men, such as fear God, men of truth, hating covetousness; and place such over them, to be rulers of thousands, and rulers of hundreds, rulers of fifties, and rulers of tens: 22 And let them judge the people at all seasons: and it shall be, that every great matter they shall bring unto thee, but every small matter they shall judge: so shall it be easier for thyself, and they shall bear the burden with thee. 23 If thou shalt do this thing, and God command thee so, then thou shalt be able to endure, and all this people shall also go to their place in peace. 24 So Moses hearkened to the voice of his father-in-law, and did all that he had said.

During his visit, Jethro noticed that Moses spent the entire day judging the people. At that time, Moses was the only person serving in that capacity. Jethro recognized that Moses' actions were detrimental to his health and to the health of the people. Moses would not be able to sustain this role. Moses needed to focus on his primary responsibility of representing the people of Israel before God. In addition to Moses teaching the people God's laws, Jethro suggested that Moses delegate some of his judging responsibility to others so those people would share the burden with Moses. The others would be responsible for small matters, while Moses would decide the more important matters. Moses used wisdom and followed the direction of his father-in-law.

DISCUSSION

1. Why is it important for family members to encourage one another?
2. How can we recognize when we are given good advice?
3. How do we know when we should encourage someone?

4. What characteristics did Jethro possess that caused Moses to follow his advice?
5. Why was it important for Moses to delegate authority to other judges?
6. Why did Jethro rejoice about all God had done for the people of Israel?

PRACTICAL APPLICATION
PERSONAL APPLICATION
1. Write a poem that reflects the relationship between Moses and Jethro.

2. Recall a time in your life when you needed encouragement or assistance from someone who had more wisdom and experience than you. How did you respond when someone gave you words of encouragement or demonstrated their support of you? Think of ways you can encourage others who need to know someone cares. Consider how you can help someone who is overwhelmed by work or other matters.

COMMUNITY APPLICATION
1. Speak with the New Members Committee or the ministry that works with new members of the church to identify ways in which you can help. You may want to join the ministry or regularly assist after speaking with someone and volunteering.

2. See if there is a community day or partnership that allows your church and the surrounding community to partner and offer encouragement and hope to others. If there is already a committee, then volunteer; if not, ask if there is an opportunity for collaboration and celebration.

Serve on the first committee for this celebration of those who encourage and give hope to others.

MEDITATION

Encouragement gives hope. It is God's desire that family members encourage one another. When we are in distress or need guidance, it is the duty of the members of our families to bring light to the situation. Often, it becomes difficult for us to make important changes in our lives because we are too close to the issues, situations, or circumstances. We may need someone with a different perspective to look at our options with wisdom and objectivity. Wisdom and objectivity can help us analyze the options in ways that we would not have been able to do without the clarity of judgment. Conversely, when our loved ones need guidance, we must behave accordingly. Studying God's Word will give us the wisdom to receive encouragement in the spirit in which it is given. The Bible and experience will give us discernment to know when others need encouragement and the wisdom to encourage appropriately.

PRAYER

Lord, we thank You for the opportunity to pray. We ask that You give us the words to encourage others so their actions will bring glory and honor to You. We ask that You give us receptive ears and hearts to receive encouragement when we need it. We thank You for the hope we receive through encouragement. We pray this in the name of Jesus, amen.

BIBLIOGRAPHY
Adeyemo, Tokunboh, ed. *Africa Bible Commentary.* Nairobi, Kenya: WordAlive Publishers, 2006.
www.BibleGateway.com

3

Forgiveness? Why?

LESSON SCRIPTURE
GENESIS 27:34–35, 41–45; 33:1–4

BACKGROUND SCRIPTURES
Genesis 25:21-34; Genesis 27-33; Malachi 1:2; Romans 9:10-18
Hebrews 11:20, 12:16

QUESTION
Recall a time when someone cheated you out of something that was rightfully yours. Describe how you felt and the emotions you experienced. Could you have forgiven that person then, and have you forgiven that person now?

HOW COULD HE HAVE DONE THAT?
An 18-year-old religion major had an assignment to write a research paper for his conducting class. He chose to write about hymn stories. He produced an excellent paper featuring stories of how God-inspired authors wrote their hymns and the impact certain hymns had on the spiritual lives of others. He was fascinated by the encounters of some of these authors and put his all into it. His paper was so well done that his teacher told other students about it.

A fellow ministerial student approached him with a request to read the paper. He took the paper and never returned it. He later submitted the paper in another class, as if it were his own work. He cheated the author of the only copy of his work. Moreover, when he graduated and began ministry, he duplicated the paper and gave it to members of the church as his Christmas gift. He neither acknowledged the original author nor gave him credit for even the idea behind the work. How could he have done that, especially as a minister? Would you have forgiven him? The author vowed not to forgive him for stealing his work. The young pastor, who stole the paper, did not learn; later in life he stole money from the church where he was a pastor.

DISCUSSION

Is cheating acceptable behavior for Christians? Are there occasions when it is acceptable to cheat just a little bit? How would you react to a Christian who decided to steal food to feed the poor and homeless in a depressed neighborhood? Also, who hurts most when we withhold forgiveness from one who has injured us?

TRANSITION

We see from this story that it is important to develop healthy habits since they follow us through life. Today's lesson teaches that despite the poor choices, habits and practices of others, it is necessary for us to forgive. We must treat others as God treats us, taking our cue from the model prayer in which we ask God to forgive us as we forgive those who trespass against us. And, the forgiver benefits more than the forgiven.

SCRIPTURE VOCABULARY

Birthright — The special rights and privileges accorded to the firstborn of any father. This meant that the firstborn inherited two portions—double the portions received by the other males (females inherited only when there were no males). The rights of the firstborn also included leadership among the other brothers after the death of the father.

Blessing — Pronouncements that variously solicit, distribute, and celebrate well-being. While this refers generally to the divine favors bestowed on humans, there was a specific sense in which "godly men under inspiration bestowed prophetic blessings on their progeny . . . as Isaac blessed Jacob and Esau".

Firstborn — Denotes the firstborn to come out of the womb, especially of humans particularly, but not exclusively, who were dedicated to God because He "reserved [them] to himself" in a special way. Among the Hebrews, the firstborn son possessed special rights and privileges. He succeeded his father as the head of the house and received as his share of the inheritance a double portion.

Forgiveness — "The act of ceasing to feel resentment towards an offender," especially when his or her actions deserve it. It is the generous abandonment of all desire to pursue retaliation for a wrong sustained. It is the liberal bestowal of gifts of compassion, liberality, friendship, and grace when the offender is undeserving of anything other than cruelty, spite, meanness, animosity, and unkindness.

SCRIPTURE REFERENCE

Genesis 27:34-35, 41-45; 33:1-4

27:34 And when Esau heard the words of his father, he cried with a great and exceeding bitter cry, and said unto his father, Bless me, even me also, O my father.

35 And he said, Thy brother came with subtilty, and hath taken away thy blessing.

27:41 And Esau hated Jacob because of the blessing wherewith his father blessed him: and Esau said in his heart, The days of mourning for my father are at hand; then will I slay my brother Jacob.

42 And these words of Esau her elder son were told to Rebekah: and she sent and called Jacob her younger son, and said unto him, Behold, thy brother Esau, as touching thee, doth comfort himself, purposing to kill thee.

43 Now therefore, my son, obey my voice; arise, flee thou to Laban my brother to Haran;

44 And tarry with him a few days, until thy brother's fury turn away;

45 Until thy brother's anger turn away from thee, and he forget that which thou hast done to him: then I will send, and fetch thee from thence: why should I be deprived also of you both in one day?

33:1 And Jacob lifted up his eyes, and looked, and, behold, Esau came, and with him four hundred men. And he divided the children unto Leah, and unto Rachel, and unto the two handmaids.

2 And he put the handmaids and their children foremost, and Leah and her children after, and Rachel and Joseph hindermost.

3 And he passed over before them, and bowed himself to the ground seven times, until he came near to his brother.

4 And Esau ran to meet him, and embraced him, and fell on his neck, and kissed him: and they wept.

MEMORY VERSE

"Be ye kind one to another, tenderhearted, forgiving one another" (from Ephesians 4:32).

HOW DOES THE MEMORY VERSE APPLY TO YOUR FAITH WALK?

_____

_____

_____

_____

LESSON FOCUS

This lesson invites us to reflect on the implications of our actions and how they affect others and relate to God's grand scheme. Esau regarded his birthright lightly; Isaac neglected to follow God's stated plan; Rebekah deliberately chose to be contrary to Isaac's stated wishes, but had God's promise as her overarching principle; and Jacob questioned his mother's plan but went along with it anyway. Perhaps he had developed ambitions based on the stories he heard about God's promise. No matter Jacob's thoughts, the pride of deception led to deeper family problems. Eventually, we discover through this biblical story that in spite of playing the "favorite game," forgiveness and God's plan still prevailed.

BIBLE BACKGROUND

Our story is set in patriarchal times, about 19 centuries before the life of Jesus of Nazareth. Isaac and his relatives are Bedouins living in the land of Canaan. Though they are primarily shepherds who live off the land, they would be viewed as wealthy by ancient standards as well as by modern considerations because of their many possessions. Possession of cows, donkeys, horses, goats, and sheep indicated power and wealth (_Anchor Bible,_ 1187). They needed help with the flocks, so there were two kinds of shepherds: owner shepherds like Abraham, Isaac, and Jacob, and hired shepherds who tended the flocks of others. That is why Jesus said He was the good shepherd and not a hireling who would flee in the face of danger (see John 10:11–13).

Jacob was a hired shepherd to Laban. Archaeology has confirmed that in the Ancient Near East, the shepherding cycle lasted seven years. This confirms the biblical account that Jacob worked seven years for Leah, and when he got Leah, he pledged to work another seven years to get Rachel. He worked 14 years total for both of them. He then contracted to work for another seven years for wages but left in the sixth year of that contract. Thus, he worked a total of 20 years for Laban. Refer to Genesis 31:38–41 in which Jacob tells Laban precisely this.

The setting is interesting. Rebekah was barren and remained childless for a long time. This means that Esau and Jacob came later in life for both parents. Genesis 25:26 says Isaac was 60 years old at their birth. At the time of the story in Genesis 27, Isaac is old and blind, and considers himself near death—even though he lived for more than 20 years after this story took place. He lived for several years thereafter, even to see the return of Jacob from Padanaram.

The birthright is the prerogative of the firstborn child. Yet, we see Jacob's interest in the birthright while Esau is nonchalant about it. Perhaps Rebekah told Jacob what the Lord told her. It could also be that Esau's disinterest is based on the stories he, too, had heard. We must not underrate the function of stories in the development and nurturing of children.

SCRIPTURE EXPLORATION

Genesis 27:34-35— And when Esau heard the words of his father, he cried with a great and exceeding bitter cry, and said unto his father, Bless me, even me also, O my father. 35 And he said, Thy brother came with subtilty,

and hath taken away thy blessing.

Many readers look at the rivalry between Jacob and Esau for the birthright and conclude that Jacob was an ambitious and pushy fellow who did everything to get the blessing that was rightfully his brother's. Perhaps he was, but this approach bypasses the intrigue and human interests involved in the story. Jacob was not the only guilty party in this situation. In fact, this passage serves as an interesting case study in human behavior as well as in psychological development.

Jacob and Esau are the products of prayer. Rebekah was barren and Isaac prayed for her, asking God to take away her disgrace and allow her to conceive. And He did (Genesis 25:21). Like some mothers, she had a difficult pregnancy. She could not understand what was happening in her womb—there was frequent, inexplicable jostling taking place. She consulted God for an explanation. God told her, "Two nations *are in your womb,* and two peoples from within you will be separated; one people will be stronger than the other, and the older will serve the younger" (Genesis 25:22–23). This lets us know that the problems we see outworking in Genesis 25 and 27 between Jacob and Esau actually began prenatally.

Genesis 25:24–25 confirms the veracity of God's words to Rebekah. She actually gave birth to twins. Verse 26 highlights the continued saga between the boys. They were completely unalike—Esau was red and hairy and Jacob was smooth-skinned. The younger brother, Jacob, came out of the womb grasping on to the heel of his elder brother, Esau. Also, Esau loved the open fields and became a hunter while Jacob was a home-loving boy (verse 27). One would have suspected that, given what began prenatally and given the heads-up God had given them, Isaac and Rebekah would have been careful in their nurture of the boys. However, this proved to be only wishful thinking. Genesis 25:28 says each parent had a favorite child. Isaac loved Esau, especially for his venison, and Rebekah loved Jacob. This was indeed a recipe for disaster.

The rights and privileges of the firstborn were known and respected among the ancients. As the firstborn, Esau owned the birthright and should have received it with the family blessing and all else that was involved. Yet, he showed utter disrespect for it, as Genesis 25:29–34 highlights. Whether or not Rebekah had told the children, especially Jacob, about the predictive Word of the Lord, we are not told. What we do know is that one day, Jacob cooked soup and Esau came in hungry and requested some; kinship could not prevail and make Jacob share his food to relieve the hunger of his famished brother. Rather, he bartered and got the birthright from Esau as payment for the food to relieve his hunger. Note how the author of Hebrews renders it: "Lest there be any fornicator, or profane person, as Esau, who for one morsel of meat sold his birthright" (Hebrews 12:16).

Genesis 27:41-45—And Esau hated Jacob because of the blessing wherewith his father blessed him: and Esau said in his heart, The days of mourning for my father are at hand; then will I slay my brother Jacob. 42 And these words of Esau her elder son were told to Rebekah: and she sent and called Jacob her younger son, and said unto him, Behold, thy brother Esau, as touching thee, doth comfort himself, purposing to kill thee. 43 Now therefore, my son, obey my voice; arise, flee thou to Laban my brother to Haran; 44 And tarry with him a few days, until thy brother's fury turn away; 45 Until thy brother's anger turn away from thee, and he forget that which thou hast done to him: then I will send, and fetch thee from thence: why should I be deprived also of you both in one day?

Despite what God had revealed to Rebekah concerning the future of the children, Genesis 27:1 says Isaac decided to go ahead of God and give the family blessing to Esau, his favorite son. Instead of confronting Isaac with the Word of God, Rebekah devised a scheme by which Jacob deceived his father to receive the blessing. Although Jacob was a reluctant participant in the scheme, he cooperated anyway. The words of Isaac, "The voice is Jacob's voice, but the hands are the hands of Esau" are fascinating and highlight the fact that although Isaac was suspicious, he was convinced enough to think it was actually Esau receiving his blessing. Yet, in reality, the recipient of the blessing was actually Jacob. Esau arrived too late for the blessing; his wail was also too late. He neither knew nor appreciated what he had until he lost it.

What this review reveals is that all four family members were caught in the web of deception. Isaac deceived himself into thinking he could deceive God and Rebekah and give the blessing to Esau. Rebekah deceived Isaac into blessing Jacob, trying to help God in fulfilling His plan. Jacob deceived his father into thinking he was Esau and stole the blessing that was intended for his brother. Esau deceived himself into thinking that the birthright meant nothing to him until he discovered he had lost it, as well as the blessing. What is very intriguing here is the role the parents played in this web of deception while still claiming to be servants of God. Here they again deceived themselves, their children, and the world, but not God.

Actions like these never go unpunished. Esau would not forgive Jacob and vowed to kill him (Genesis 27:41). Through another scheme, Rebekah had him shipped away to Padanaram where, in a twist of fate, Jacob is deceived and cheated several times by his uncle. Isaac and Rebekah lost both Jacob and Esau. Jacob had to run away to save his life and Esau went away, making his life one of spite for his parents (Genesis 28:6–9). This shows unforgiveness toward them. Isaac and Jacob experienced at least a 20-year separation, and there is no further record of interaction between Jacob and Rebekah. So, we are unsure whether they ever saw each other again. It appears that they did not. This must have been painful for this family, but it shows us the pitfalls of favoritism and teaches us to avoid this curse in the training and nurturing of our own children.

> **Genesis 33:1-4—And Jacob lifted up his eyes, and looked, and, behold, Esau came, and with him four hundred men. And he divided the children unto Leah, and unto Rachel, and unto the two handmaids. 2 And he put the handmaids and their children foremost, and Leah and her children after, and Rachel and Joseph hindermost. 3 And he passed over before them, and bowed himself to the ground seven times, until he came near to his brother. 4 And Esau ran to meet him, and embraced him, and fell on his neck, and kissed him: and they wept.**

Thankfully, this is not the end of the story. Twenty years later, on his return flight to Canaan, we see what began as a heated argument between Jacob and his Esau (33:4) ending in forgiveness, reconciliation, and renewal. We also see forgiveness and restoration of relations between Jacob and God at the Brook Jabbok. He receives a blessing and a change of name from Jacob to Israel. Consider what Jacob's relationship with Esau was like: Esau stole from him, Jacob left home because of a death threat. No wonder Jacob was terrified when he heard Esau was on his way to meet him. Those wounds must have festered for both of them over those years. How wonderful then to see what we encounter in the text. "Esau ran to meet him, and embraced him, and fell on his neck, and kissed him: and they wept" (Genesis 33:4). Imagine the relief this must have brought! The chapter even tells of Jacob giving gifts to Esau (verses 8–11) and of meaningful conversation between them. Moreover, Esau proposed that they travel home together from their meeting point. Although his offer was not accepted, it was a good gesture and Jacob's refusal did not create a breach in their new-found relations. There was forgiveness and reconciliation.

Can you imagine the relief this pleasant meeting must have brought after 20 years of hatred, animosity, and bitterness? Can you image the freedom that forgiveness gave both Jacob and Esau? The same forgiveness also took place between Jacob and Isaac (Genesis 35:27). When Isaac finally died at age 180, both brothers united to bury him (Genesis 35:29). This was a great development!

DISCUSSION

1. What is the most valuable lesson you learned from the story?
2. How should parents deal with sibling rivalries? Share an incident you've had with your children as they were growing up and how you dealt with it.
3. If you were Rebekah and you saw Isaac acting contrary to the divine plan for the children, how would you have dealt with the situation? What course of action would you have followed?
4. How difficult do you find the grace of forgiveness? Is

there an easy way around it? Share with the class how you cope with following the injunction to treat others with forgiveness, kindness, and tenderheartedness.

5. Who benefits most from forgiveness—the forgiver or the forgiven? Please explain and be able to defend your answer with Scriptures and examples. Discuss the benefits of forgiveness for body and soul.

6. A famous British general once said, "I never forgive!" Why is this a very unfortunate statement? What counsel would you give him and why?

PRACTICAL APPLICATION
PERSONAL APPLICATION

1. Your firstborn, a girl, understands and imbibes all the values and virtues the family has taught her. Her brother, on the other hand, is rebellious and tries to get away with as much as possible. You discover that your son has begun to resent his sister and the resentment is becoming physical because he thinks she is a conformist and a tattletale. How would you resolve this conflict, preserving your daughter's understanding while addressing your son's rebellion and the sibling rivalry, all without alienating either child? Demonstrate forgiveness with and for them both.

2. Francis Bacon once said, "In taking revenge a man is but even with his enemy; but in passing it over he is superior, for it is a prince's part to pardon." Do you agree with Bacon? If so, why? If not, why not? How would you apply this notion to your daily life?

COMMUNITY APPLICATION

1. Your church has some unused land on which community children have been playing. Some members of the trustee board feel that this is inappropriate use of church property. They erect a "no trespassing" sign on the property. The children feel rejected, trash the church property, and even take some items. What process would you recommend to bring about healing and restoration? Using your plan as a starting point, facilitate a discussion on how to restore trust between the church, the children, and the community.

2. Two brothers partnered and purchased 100 acres of prime land in an area marked for future development. After the deal, one brother divided the land and took the frontage portion—40 acres, which was the best part for himself, leaving the back wooded area for his brother. What would you have done if were you the brother left with the back wooded area? How would you resolve this blatant act of cheating and injustice between the brothers?

3. You are part of a large family that has been feuding for years over a property that was bequeathed to the family members, but not distributed in a manner all thought was fair and equitable. There are expressed desires for resolution, but all members are too proud to accept it. Devise a plan that would resolve the feud and demonstrate how you would implement it.

MEDITATION

Family is one of the closest thing on earth to heaven. God has given us this entity to nurture the next generation; teach the virtues, qualities, and character required for life above; and help us develop the graces and socialization necessary to live with saints and heavenly beings. Because we are so diverse, we appreciate things, and each other, differently. It is natural for us to offend and irritate each other. Yet, just as we protect a broken toe or a hurt finger or eye rather than cutting them off and discarding them, so we should neither cut off nor discard irritating family members. We need them and they need us. At times, they are placed there to help us demonstrate our heavenly graces.

We are all interconnected. We are all pilgrims on the path to heaven. We need one another. We are not competitors. We complement and complete each other. We all can win and it is not a "one-winner-take-all" affair. Therefore, we can be kind to one another, tenderhearted and forgiving of each other, and we can extend these graces and still win the race. Ultimately, we are expected to reciprocate with others what the Master has done to and for us.

PRAYER

Dear Lord, the universe is so vast and my craft is so small. Teach me the value of family. Help me understand that the bumps and bruises of family life and interpersonal relations are designed to help me grow. Help me appreciate the blessings of family, friends, and church. Help me to be true to myself and to You by refraining from cheating or misrepresenting another. Help me to realize that I don't hurt others when I refuse to forgive; I hurt myself. Help me, therefore, to extend forgiveness to others and to be kind and gentle to all I meet. Amen!

BIBLIOGRAPHY

Alexander, Desmond T. and David W. Baker. *Dictionary of the Old Testament: Pentateuch*.
    Downers Grove, IL: Intervarsity Press, 2003.

Freeman, David N., ed., *The Anchor Bible Dictionary,* 6 Vols. New York: Doubleday, 1992.

The Holy Bible, King James Version.

Nave, Orville J. *Nave's Topical Bible*. Peabody, MA: Hendrickson Publishers, 1988.

Sakenfeld, Kathrine D. *The New Interpreter's Dictionary of the Bible*, 5 Vols. Nashville: Abingdon
    Press, 2007. p. 471, 477, 457-458.

Tenney, Merryl, ed., *The Zondervan Pictorial Bible Dictionary*. Grand Rapids, MI: Zondervan
    Publishing House, 1967. p. 127, 283.

Webster's II New College Dictionary. Houghton Mifflin, 1995.

4

Protecting Family

LESSON SCRIPTURE
GENESIS 14:11-20

BACKGROUND SCRIPTURES
Genesis 12:4, 13:1-18, 14, 19; 1 Corinthians 13:7; 1 Timothy 5:4;
2 Peter 2:6-8

QUESTION
What risks are you willing to take and what strength do you draw on to protect someone in your church family and biological family?

FAMILY TO THE RESCUE
Janie was introduced to Jesus Christ by her coworker and began attending her neighborhood church. She completed her new member classes and became part of the Communications Ministry. Everyone enjoyed Janie and her service to the church and the ministry; she did excellent work. After about six months, a member in the ministry told Janie a rumor was spreading about her past substance abuse problem. When she heard that, Janie was devastated: first, because most of the information was awful and untrue, and second, because she thought people in the church were different or better than to spread gossip. The event caused Janie to become distraught, withdrawn, and perplexed about whether to continue attending the church or not. She told the problem to the president of the

Communications Ministry, who went with Janie to report the problem to the pastor.

DISCUSSION
Have you ever had to help someone whose name and reputation was ruined or tainted? Whether the information was true or not, how did you respond? In the story, what risk did the Communications Ministry president take? What other actions could have been taken in Janie's dilemma?

TRANSITION
Courage, love, and faith in God are essential factors in this story, as well as in the Abram story of this lesson. There are situations beyond our control that place our family members in danger, yet we are called to the rescue. Just as there were driving factors that led the Communications Ministry president to rescue a spiritual family member, Abram's faith in God and love for his family led him to risk his life to rescue his nephew, Lot, from powerful oppressors. His nephew's exercise of poor judgment and lack of respect for his uncle did not keep Abram from doing what was necessary to save Lot and others. This lesson is all about a family affair and gives us the opportunity to dissect all the elements involved in protecting our family members no matter where they are—in our home, our places of worship, or in faraway places. This Bible story lets us know that rescuing our family often requires the same kind of faith that Abram displayed in being obedient to the only true God who is a "strong tower."

SCRIPTURE VOCABULARY
Victuals — Food and food preparation required by the body to sustain life. The availability of food was a perpetual concern because of the recurrent scarcity

due to frequent drought. Farming was frequently
interrupted by warfare with neighboring nations.

Mamre — A town 20 miles south of Jerusalem named for
one of Abram's friends.

Confederate — Allies (ESV), which means a relationship
between parties.

Most High — Translation of a Hebrew (*'ēl 'ēlyon*) name for
God. It was used in place of Yahweh in Genesis 14:22.

SCRIPTURE REFERENCE

GENESIS 14:11-20

11 *And they took all the goods of Sodom and Gomorrah, and
all their victuals, and went their way.*

12 *And they took Lot, Abram's brother's son, who dwelt in
Sodom, and his goods, and departed.*

13 *And there came one that had escaped, and told Abram the
Hebrew; for he dwelt in the plain of Mamre the Amorite,
brother of Eshcol, and brother of Aner: and these were
confederate with Abram.*

14 *And when Abram heard that his brother was taken captive,
he armed his trained servants, born in his own house, three
hundred and eighteen, and pursued them unto Dan.*

15 *And he divided himself against them, he and his servants,
by night, and smote them, and pursued them unto Hobah,
which is on the left hand of Damascus.*

16 *And he brought back all the goods, and also brought again
his brother Lot, and his goods, and the women also, and
the people.*

17 *And the king of Sodom went out to meet him after his return
from the slaughter of Chedorlaomer, and of the kings that
were with him, at the valley of Shaveh, which is the king's
dale.*

18 And Melchizedek king of Salem brought forth bread and wine: and he was the priest of the most high God.

19 And he blessed him, and said, Blessed be Abram of the most high God, possessor of heaven and earth:

20 And blessed be the most high God, which hath delivered thine enemies into thy hand. And he gave him tithes of all.

MEMORY VERSE

"The name of the LORD is a strong tower: the righteous runneth into it, and is safe" (Proverbs 18:10).

HOW DOES THE MEMORY VERSE APPLY TO YOUR FAITH WALK?

_____

_____

_____

_____

_____

LESSON FOCUS

We come face to face with what happens when a family member is in a helpless situation because one who is stronger has taken advantage of him. This Scripture passage shows that God is not blind to the oppression of those under His protection and will use ordinary people to do extraordinary things. Knowing this, we are able to rescue members of our biological family and our spiritual family who may be in danger of physical or spiritual harm. Abram helps readers of this Scripture passage consider the importance of being obedient and faithful to God's call to protect the family and know that planning, courage, and sacrifice are all part of the process.

BIBLE BACKGROUND

The events of our Scripture passage take place between 2000 and 1500 B.C. in the second part of Genesis (Chapters 12-50), which begins the discussion of the patriarchs (Abraham—the name God gave to Abram—Isaac, and Jacob) of Israel (*Chronological Study Bible*, 2008, 19).

Abram and his father lived in Ur of the Chaldees. It was a major city known for its huge temple-tower, called a ziggurat, which was used for worship of various gods. Perhaps the history of this imposing structure and others like it influenced Solomon's writing of our Memory Verse in Proverbs 18:10 describing God as a "strong tower."

Abram and Sarai, his half-sister and wife, and Lot, his nephew, moved northward with Abram's father, Terah, to Haran. According to Zondervan's Illustrated Bible Dictionary, Haran was an important commercial city because its location between Babylonia and the Mediterranean (1987, 574). Haran was a commercially and culturally important center in the early history of the Hebrew nation.

Abram's Call

While Abram was in Haran, God told him to move to another place. That is, the calling of Abram—the beginning of the nation of Israel—is a story of tremendous significance. (*Opening up Genesis Commentary*, 2009, 60–61). Abram's obedience was being tested in his call to leave his hometown and go to another place, especially when he had no clue as to where he was going. Furthermore, he had to provide for not only himself, but also for his wife, his nephew, Lot (Abram's deceased brother's son), and all the people who worked for him. In spite of these concerns, Abram obeyed God's call and took his family and servants out of Haran to the outskirts of Canaan to the plains of Moreh, a place near Sichem. It was at this place that God promised

Abram that his descendants would own the land where he was then located. Acknowledging the presence of the Lord, Abram built an altar.

Abram, with his family, moved further to the hill country, where he built another altar and worshiped the Lord. Abram continued his journey southward and encountered what in today's world, would be considered a recession. So Abram did what many people are doing in today's economy: he took his family to another location—Egypt—where he and his family could live comfortably. After a series of events, Abram was sent away from Egypt (see Genesis 12:11-20) and in Chapter 13, it is recorded that Abram returned to Bethel, the place where he first built an altar to the Lord. In fact, Abram built three altars. Each time God appeared to Abram, this act of worship took place.

Lot's Indiscretions

A family feud began between Abram's and Lot's workers. By now, Lot had accumulated some wealth. He had a large number of livestock and tents, but the land was not big enough for both Lot and Abram. To further complicate matters, the land was also occupied by the Canaanites and the Perizzites. Later we come to know them as a people of abominable behavior and capable of significant influence on the people of God (Ezra 9:1). To abate the feud and keep peace in the family, Abram offered Lot the first opportunity to choose which part of the land he preferred, indicating that what Lot did not choose, Abram would. This leadership attribute displayed by Abram is a godly example of resolving conflict. Lot chose the best for himself after seeing an area that was the most fertile, with more than enough water for his cattle and large areas to set up his tents.

Lot traveled to the east, near Sodom and Gomorrah, to set up his residence. Lot made this choice without regard for the likely exposure of himself and his workers to the evil surroundings.

His indiscretion and selfishness surface in his choice of the area in which he would set up his tents. We will see eventually that Lot's decision placed his family and all his possessions in danger.

Abram Moves Again

Yielding to Lot's desire, Abram moved to the plains of Mamre, and Lot moved to the cities near Sodom. After Abram separated from Lot and arrived in the new location, God appeared to Abram again and promised him even more land and innumerable descendants. So there in Hebron, in the plain of Mamre, Abram built another altar to the Lord.

The Continuing Battle of Power

Amraphel, king of Shinar; Arioch, king of Ellasar; Chedorlaomer, king of Elam; and Tidal, king of nations (Genesis 14:1), are the four kings of the east who formed a coalition of strength in the land of Israel at that time. This was not uncommon because there were many alliances and power struggles between the city-states of Middle Bronze Age Palestine during that time. (Knowles, 2001, 30). In fact, on the way to fight the four kings of the west, they fought against and took over six other areas. Chedorlaomer appears to be the leading king in this Scripture because his name appears either first or by itself (Genesis 14:4, 5, 9). He and the other kings could be characterized in today's terms as the bullies of east, requiring the kings of the west to pay tribute to them. The kings of the west were Bera, king of Sodom; Birsha, king of Gommorah; Shinab, king of Admah; Shemeber, king of Zeboiim; and the king of Bela (no name given). These five kings were overtaken by the four kings of the east and were required to pay an annual tribute to keep the kings from taking their goods and their people. For 12 years, the western kings did just that—they paid the kings what they wanted.

By the 13th year, the kings of the west refused to pay (Genesis 14:2-4). The next year, the 14th year, Chedorlaomer and his allies fought everyone in their region and took their possessions. The kings of the west could not stand up to the strength and might of Chedorlaomer and his coalition during this war. Their plight is emblematic of the rich taking advantage of the poor, the strong overcoming the weak. The western kings were defeated (Genesis 14:10).

SCRIPTURE EXPLORATION

> *Genesis 14:11-12—And they took all the goods of Sodom and Gomorrah, and all their victuals, and went their way. 12 And they took Lot, Abram's brother's son, who dwelt in Sodom, and his goods, and departed.*

The "they" in verse 11 refers to the eastern kings— Chedorlaomer and the others with him—who conquered the cities of Sodom and Gomorrah, took everything of value from them—including their food supplies—and went on their way. It is interesting to note that even though there were three other cities involved, Sodom and Gomorrah are the only two mentioned. They are known for the wickedness of their people (Genesis 13:13; 18:23, 25), who live in rebellion to God. These are the people over whom the eastern kings prevailed, taking away their people and possessions, including Lot, Abram's nephew, and all his possessions.

Unlike Abram, Lot aligned himself with evil people by choosing to live in Sodom and was captured by the eastern kings. He was in the wrong place at the wrong time. His choice of that particular location was lawful for him but not expedient (1 Corinthians 6:12). It was not expedient because the evil environment he chose was in stark contradiction to Abram's choices in the several moves they made together. Lot overlooked the evil and failed to depart from it (Proverbs 13:19), being overcome by the powerful beauty of the surroundings. As a result of his foolish choice, Lot suffered the consequence of his decision and is made to face his poor judgment.

While Lot was with Abram, he was covered under the blessings of God to Abram, but when he went off on his own, Lot "forfeited the divine protection provided by the favored patriarch" (*New American Commentary*, 2005, 140). Lot chose a different path than that of his uncle and proved that the grass is not necessarily greener on the other side and that from the outside, one is unable to determine the inner workings of a place or person. Lot connected himself to a place where the king had no concept of what godly leadership meant, very unlike the environment in which he grew up.

Genesis 14:13-16—And there came one that had escaped, and told Abram the Hebrew; for he dwelt in the plain of Mamre the Amorite, brother of Eshcol, and brother of Aner: and these were confederate with Abram. 14 And when Abram heard that his brother was taken captive, he armed his trained servants, born in his own house, three hundred and eighteen, and pursued them unto Dan. 15 And he divided himself against them, he and his servants, by night, and smote them, and pursued them unto Hobah, which is on the left hand of Damascus. 16 And he brought back all the goods, and also brought again his brother Lot, and his goods, and the women also, and the people.

The news of Lot's capture came to Abram from one of the people who escaped from the eastern kings. This messenger was a Sodomite who knew that Abram was Lot's uncle. He knew where Abram lived and he knew Abram as the Hebrew. Use of this genealogical term to identify Abram indicates that Abram was true to his God and was of good character. To be called a Hebrew at that time was to be linked with "Heber, in whose family the profession of true religion was kept up" (*Matthew Henry Commentary* on Genesis 13-16). Abram had, no doubt, attained a reputation among the non-Hebrew people in the region for being a trusted ally. People in the surrounding area knew him and his love for his family. They became his confederates. This unnamed messenger believed Abram would rescue his own nephew and, perhaps, some of the messenger's people.

Abram sprung into action. He knew the strength of the eastern kings and he also knew the strength of his God, who promised him the land and the people in it. With those two elements in mind, he called his servants to become the army that would help rescue his nephew. Abram knew he would encounter opposition from those who had proven to be very powerful forces by taking away the wealth of five cities, but he was willing to take the risk to save his family. So he led his small army of 318 men to victory, much like Gideon, who was victorious with only 300 men out of 32,000 (Judges 7:7). With the power of God and a plan of attack, Abram won the battle. His plan for a night attack rendered the opposition helpless, and he was able to overtake them and rescue his nephew, his family, all his possessions, and all the people.

Genesis 14:17-20—And the king of Sodom went out to meet him after his return from the slaughter of Chedorlaomer, and of the kings that were with him, at the valley of Shaveh, which is the king's dale. 18 And Melchizedek king of Salem brought forth bread

and wine: and he was the priest of the most high God.
19 And he blessed him, and said, Blessed be Abram of
the most high God, possessor of heaven and earth: 20
And blessed be the most high God, which hath delivered
thine enemies into thy hand. And he gave him tithes of
all.

After Abram's victory over the eastern kings, he was visited
by Bera, the king of Sodom. This is the only place in the Bible
where this king is mentioned, so we know very little about him.
We do know his city was evil, with no record of his attempts to
change its reputation. Did Bera come to Abram to congratulate
him? Before we can answer that question, we are introduced
to Melchizedek, king of Salem (a name for Jerusalem in Psalm
76:2). Notice the parallel between the two kings:

- Bera, king of Sodom, an evil city

- Melchizedek, king of Salem, a holy city

This tells the story of these two very different leaders and
their expected ends: one will be forever destroyed, the other
forever exalted.

Melchizedek brought sustenance for Abram and for those
in his house. This is Melchizedek's way of showing gratitude
to Abram and his army for righting the wrongs done to the
people by their enemies. As well, to bring nourishment after
a battle is a way to comfort those who have traveled far and
fought hard (Genesis 18:5). In addition to the bread and wine,
Melchizedek blessed Abram. Melchizedek is already identified
as the priest of the most high God, and he blessed Abram in the
name of the most high God (Hebrews 7:6). By their actions, both
Melchizedek and Abram agreed that amidst the fear and risk
involved in rescuing Lot from this powerful army of the four

kings, only God could provide enough courage, strength, and determination to intercede on Lot's behalf. In acknowledgment of God's blessings, Abram gives one-tenth of all the wealth he obtained from the battle as an offering to God (Micah 6:6).

The one-tenth represents the "tithes," which are mentioned in this passage for the first time in the Scriptures. This act of giving in Genesis 14:20 demonstrates to the reader that the tithe is freely given because of God's many blessings. This offering of one-tenth after Abram's victory acknowledges that when evil people take what is not theirs, God will provide the courage godly people need to go, rescue, and restore. God, who is most high over all the earth (Psalms 83:18), can deliver God's people from all challenges and did deliver Lot through Abram. Abram then blessed God for it.

Abram and Melchizedek are examples of what it means to bless God for victory over evil done to the people; in this case, not only Abram's biological family but others who were in danger.

DISCUSSION

1. What, in Abram's response to God's call to move to another place, speaks to you? That is, how can you know when God speaks to you, and how did or would you respond to God's call to go? Provide an example.

2. We know Abram was closely aligned with God. They had several encounters in which God promised Abram he would possess the land, including the places where these events were taking place. Is it possible that Abram's thoughts were on his nephew as well as on protecting the land the Lord promised? Explain your response.

3. How did Abram model his obedience to God regarding his biological and extended family? Are there any parallels in our society today?

4. What are some important factors to consider when choosing a place to live?
5. Abram raised Lot like his own son. Can you list some ways Lot could have demonstrated his appreciation?
6. Abram risked defeat when he took a small army to fight against the powerful kings. How does Abram's story highlight the importance of protecting the biological or spiritual family?
7. What lesson for the Christian is seen in Melchizedek's and Abram's blessing of the Lord? What did they do, and what does it teach?

PRACTICAL APPLICATION
PERSONAL APPLICATION

1. In some families, it is common to take a relative into the home when his or her parents cannot care for them because of illness, death or, more commonly, because the parents found work in another city or state. Just as Lot needed Abram to raise him after the death of his father, many foster children need permanent families to raise them. Many Christians have the time and resources to care for a child in their home. What are some other considerations needed to adopt children and assure they will receive the best possible care? Have you ever considered providing a permanent home for a child who does not have one? Abram was an excellent role model for Lot. Do you show and share the Christ in you for those who need to see God through you?

2. The saying "sticks and stones may break my bones, but words can never hurt me" has been proven inaccurate many times. Poor judgment is seen in the behaviors of those who would harm others with their words and conduct.

The silent majority in the secular and sacred community is often more harmful for not rescuing those beig harmed by words and conduct. The story of Abram teaches us that as soon as someone told him his family was in danger, he "pursued them." In light of Abram's faith in God and God's empowerment, causing Abram to defeat the powerful kings, consider being one who rescues those in your biological or spiritual family who are in danger. Then, bless God for the success you have been given.

COMMUNITY APPLICATION

Genesis 14 gives an example of how rulers took from the people for their own profit. Look around your community and notice the inequities. When you identify inequities, pray for knowledge and courage to speak truth to the power so the "least of these" can be rescued. Seek opportunities to volunteer, donate, organize, or otherwise help with programs that promote excellence in which you can teach the importance of family and the virtues of courage, loyalty, patience, and justice to youth and young adults.

MEDITATION

There are moments in our lives when we make poor choices and selfish choices that cause problems for ourselves and others. The consequences of our actions are often harsh and life changing. Yet, we serve a God who cares for us when have been selfish and may not have made the best decision. God's love reaches wider and deeper than we can imagine or know. God's love is real and true. When the Lord sends an Abram into your life to handle our foolishness, let us remember to give thanks to God and our Abram. Let us choose to concentrate on God's love and live in more excellent ways and less selfishly.

PRAYER

Dear Heavenly Father, I acknowledge Your greatness, Your love, and Your mercy. There is none like You. I pray Your forgiveness of my sins and ask for restoration to the joy of doing Your will. Thank You for this opportunity to study Your Word about Abram and the example he demonstrates through his obedience to You and his love of family. Thank You for showing me how to be a peacemaker in my family by rescuing those who are being overtaken by others stronger or more powerful than they. Help me to know how to show my love for family, whether it is in my home, my church, or my community. Teach me thy way, O Lord and lead me to a plain path so my words will be gentle and my own behavior will be as the light in darkness. Help me always to remember that You are my light and my salvation, and that I need not have any fear because You are the strength of my life and I need not be afraid of anyone or anything. Bless my home and everyone in it so all who see us will see You living in us. Strengthen my church family so we will love one another as You have commanded. In Jesus' name, I pray, amen!

BIBLIOGRAPHY

http://www.biblegateway.com/passage/?search=Genesis%2014:11-20&version=KJV (Accessed 8/27/12)

Douglas, J. D. and Teney, Merrill C. revised by Moisés Silva. Zondervan's Illustrated Bible Dictionary (Grand Rapids, MI: Zondervan, 2001).

Elwell, W. A., & Comfort, P. W. *Tyndale Bible Dictionary*. Tyndale reference library (Wheaton, IL: Tyndale House Publishers, 2001).

The Learning Bible, Contemporary English Version (New York: American Bible Society, 2000).

The ESV Study Bible, (Wheaton, IL: Crossway Bibles, 2001).

Eerdmans Dictionary of the Bible, ed. David Noel Freedman (Grand Rapids: Wm B. Eerdmans Publishing Company, 2000).

The Chronological Study Bible, NKJV (Nashville: Thomas Nelson, Inc., 2008)

Strassner, K. *Opening up Genesis*. Opening Up Commentary, Leominster: Day One Publications (2009).

Knowles, A. *The Bible Guide*, 1st Augsburg books ed. (Minneapolis, MN: Augsburg, 2001).

Mathews, K. A., *Vol. 1B: Genesis 11:27–50:26. The New American Commentary* (Nashville: Broadman & Holman Publishers 2005).

Henry, M., *Matthew Henry's Commentary on the Whole Bible: Complete and unabridged in one volume (Genesis 14:13–16)*. Peabody: Hendrickson, 1994).

5

My Jars Are Empty

LESSON SCRIPTURE
1 Kings 17:7-16

BACKGROUND SCRIPTURE
2 Kings 4; Psalm 37:19; Matthew 10:41-42, 14:13-21, 15:29-39, 16:9; Luke 4:22-26, 21:1-3; Acts 6:1-7; James 1:27

QUESTION
Have you ever given your very last to someone? If so, describe your feelings afterward.

PECAN SWIRLS
While attending college, there were often times when he didn't have money to buy food. During those times, he would somehow survive with the assistance of friends until money was sent from home or he received his work-study check. On one occasion, he received money and immediately went to the local grocery store, which was less than a block from his dormitory. When he arrived at the store, he got all the essentials a college freshman would purchase—bread, milk, cereal, Spam®, and pecan swirls.

As he left the store with his bags of groceries, he noticed a man begging for money to buy something to eat. Although he was hungry, he decided to give the man a couple of the items in his bag, including his delightful pecan swirls. As he looked back moments later, the man threw away the items he'd given him. He was hurt, angry, and hungry. As he continued back to his dorm, he thought to himself, "So much for giving! Never again!"

DISCUSSION
Once a gift is given, do you ever focus on what's done with it? Why or why not?

TRANSITION
Our story indicates that "giving" is a natural—and very often predictable—response to people or a community in need, and plays an important role in building a relationship with God. This lesson's theme, "giving," reminds us that giving sustains family and community, and strengthens our bond with God.

SCRIPTURE VOCABULARY
Elijah the Tishbite — Elijah lived in the northern kingdom of Israel in 9th century B.C. during the reign of Ahab and Jezebel. Elijah worked miracles, such as restoring a dead boy to life. He opposed the worship of the gods Baal and Astarte.

Brook Cherith — The place where Elijah hid and was fed by ravens after announcing the drought to Ahab (1 Kings 17:3-6).

Zarephath — Zarephath, which was in the region of Sidon, was the home to a widow that Elijah helped. This land is in modern-day Lebanon.

SCRIPTURE REFERENCE
1 Kings 17:7-16
7 Some time later the brook dried up because there had been no rain in the land.
8 Then the word of the Lord came to him:

9 *"Go at once to Zarephath in the region of Sidon and stay there. I have directed a widow there to supply you with food."*

10 *So he went to Zarephath. When he came to the town gate, a widow was there gathering sticks. He called to her and asked, "Would you bring me a little water in a jar so I may have a drink?"*

11 *As she was going to get it, he called, "And bring me, please, a piece of bread."*

12 *"As surely as the Lord your God lives," she replied, "I don't have any bread—only a handful of flour in a jar and a little olive oil in a jug. I am gathering a few sticks to take home and make a meal for myself and my son, that we may eat it—and die."*

13 *Elijah said to her, "Don't be afraid. Go home and do as you have said. But first make a small loaf of bread for me from what you have and bring it to me, and then make something for yourself and your son.*

14 *For this is what the Lord, the God of Israel, says: 'The jar of flour will not be used up and the jug of oil will not run dry until the day the Lord sends rain on the land.'"*

15 *She went away and did as Elijah had told her. So there was food every day for Elijah and for the woman and her family.*

16 *For the jar of flour was not used up and the jug of oil did not run dry, in keeping with the word of the Lord spoken by Elijah.*

MEMORY VERSE

"Give, and it shall be given unto you" (from Luke 6:38).

HOW DOES THE MEMORY VERSE APPLY TO YOUR FAITH WALK?

_____

_____

LESSON FOCUS

The main point of this lesson is to present "giving" as a necessary element in our reliance on God, adherence to His Word, and our faith development.

BIBLE BACKGROUND

Elijah lived in the northern kingdom of Israel in the 9th century B.C. during the reign of Ahab and Jezebel. Elijah foretells a famine for Israel as a result of its sin against God. After Elijah's communication with Ahab, God tells Elijah to hide himself by the Brook Cherith. According to the *Matthew Henry Commentary*, "This was intended, not so much for his preservation, for it does not appear that Ahab immediately sought his life, but as a judgment to the people." God did not want to place Elijah in a situation with his people in which He might feel compelled to shorten the duration of the famine. Elijah remains at the Brook Cherith until it dries up, then God sends him to Zarephath. Zarephath was located in the region of Sidon and was the home of the widow Elijah helped. She is often referred to as the "Widow of Zarephath."

SCRIPTURE EXPLORATION

1 Kings 17:7—Some time later the brook dried up because there had been no rain in the land.
The famine Elijah predicts begins. The Brook of Cherith dries

up. Nature now has to comply with the mandate or command of God. God asserts His power by stopping the rain that provides water for the brook and the life of the surrounding community. All living things, including Elijah, must now rely on God for substance.

1 Kings 17:8-9—Then the word of the Lord came to him: 9 "Go at once to Zarephath in the region of Sidon and stay there. I have directed a widow there to supply you with food."

God tells Elijah to go to Zarephath and a widow would be waiting for him there. Zarephath, in the region of Sidon, was located on the border of Israel. This area was occupied by Gentiles and was also relevant in that it was the home of Jezebel (Elijah's greatest enemy). Worship of idol gods, such as Baal, was also commonplace in Sidon. It is ironic and interesting that God would tell Elijah to go to Jezebel's hometown to find refuge and sustenance for survival, especially since Jezebel would have loved to see Elijah's life end. Yet, God would take care of Elijah where Jezebel once lived and recognized as home.

Particular notice should also be given to whom God selects to entertain Elijah. The person selected is not wealthy, well-known, or even a man. Rather, the person is a poor, single mother whom God has called to assist Elijah. This is God's way of acknowledging and restoring honor and esteem to those who appear to be weak by involving them in their healing and in the healing of others. This woman is given great value in the eyes of God and Elijah in an ancient world that discounts women and, in many cases, their importance in what was a male-dominated society.

> *1 Kings 17:10-11—So he went to Zarephath. When he came to the town gate, a widow was there gathering sticks. He called to her and asked, "Would you bring me a little water in a jar so I may have a drink?" 11 As she was going to get it, he called, "And bring me, please, a piece of bread."*

Elijah follows God's instructions; he gets up and goes to Zarephath. When he arrives, he sees the "Widow of Zarephath" gathering sticks. He asks her to bring him water and some bread. Elijah encounters the human provision selected by God for his survival. It is apparent she is much more in need of charity than she is able to provide it. Yet, Elijah does as instructed by God. Although his eyes see her obvious struggles, his faith tells him to follow the command given by God. It can be stated that, "God knows what we don't know and all he asks of us is to trust him, no matter how the situation looks."

> *1 Kings 17:12-14— "As surely as the Lord your God lives," she replied, "I don't have any bread—only a handful of flour in a jar and a little olive oil in a jug. I am gathering a few sticks to take home and make a meal for myself and my son, that we may eat it—and die." 13 Elijah said to her, "Don't be afraid. Go home and do as you have said. But first make a small loaf of bread for me from what you have and bring it to me, and then make something for yourself and your son. 14 For this is what the Lord, the God of Israel, says: 'The jar of flour will not be used up and the jug of oil will not run dry until the day the Lord sends rain on the land.'"*

The widow responds to Elijah. She says she only has enough for herself and her son, who was not a teenager but perhaps a toddler. Her intention was to cook and eat what she had; afterward, she and her son would die. Elijah states that he wants her to make his cake first and then take care of her needs and those of her son. Elijah tells her the Lord will ensure she always has meal and oil until the famine is over. After Elijah speaks these words to the widow, he then says, "for thus saith the Lord of Israel." First, this statement makes it clear to the widow that he recognizes and acknowledges the Lord of Israel as his God, even on foreign soil. As such, he will continue to serve Him, even in a strange land. Second, whether the widow is aware of the Lord of Israel or not, she is introduced to Him by Elijah. It can almost be assumed that the widow honors the name of the Lord of Israel, for she allows herself to engage in conversation regarding Elijah's God while she resides in a land where there is worship of many gods. Perhaps there is a realization that the idol gods are not able to provide for her in her time of need, but maybe the Lord of Israel can.

1 Kings 17:15-16 — She went away and did as Elijah had told her. So there was food every day for Elijah and for the woman and her family. 16 For the jar of flour was not used up and the jug of oil did not run dry, in keeping with the word of the Lord spoken by Elijah.

The widow of Zarephath does as she is told by Elijah and she always has meal and oil. She stands on the promise of God. She listens to the words of a drifter, or foreigner, whom she does not know and, as a result, addresses both their needs. She moves from hopelessness to faith and belief in what God will do for her and her son.

DISCUSSION
1. How do we promote giving in our families?

2. How is our trust in God related to how and what we give?
3. In what ways does Elijah show his trust in God?
4. What does God give to Elijah to help him physically survive the drought?
5. How does the "Widow of Zarephath" demonstrate she has trust in Elijah?
6. What physical and emotional items does the "Widow of Zarephath" give to Elijah?

PRACTICAL APPLICATION
PERSONAL APPLICATION
1. Share a kind word, perform a gracious act, or volunteer service to or for someone in the class, to be completed or scheduled by the end of the class session.

2. Write down and discuss things that inhibit your giving. Discuss with a partner or with the entire class ways in which you can overcome those obstacles.

COMMUNITY APPLICATION
1. With the assistance of others in the class, design a project for your local church that will teach children to give.

2. Develop a "Church Giving Day" initiated and facilitated by families. The goal of this day is to provide families the opportunity to offer their cleaning or repair services to special needs populations and the sick and the shut-in in the church and community.

MEDITATION
God, continue to provide us with the opportunity to give from our hearts and rejoice in You. As we give, allow us to remember to receive the joy that only You can give us. Guide

us to know how to receive blessings from others and how to give blessings to others. As we prepare our hearts and minds daily to remain open receptacles of Your wonders to behold, give us peace to sustain the journeys of life. Grant us lips of thanksgiving as You bless us to be blessings to others.

PRAYER

Thank You Lord, for being a God who supplies more than enough and sends people into our lives who help us when we are ready to give up and give in. Thank You Jesus, amen!

BIBLIOGRAPHY

http://www.bibletutor.com/level1/program/start/people/elijah.htm (1995)

Matthew Henry Commentary on the whole Bible, 1 Kings:17, http://www.studylight.org/com/mhc-com/view.cgi?book=1ki&chapter=017 (2001-2012).

6

The Gift of Love

LESSON SCRIPTURE
RUTH 1:8-9, 16-18; 4:13-17

BACKGROUND SCRIPTURES
Leviticus 19:9, 25:41-49; Numbers 5:6-8; Deuteronomy 10:18,
23:3, 24:19-22; Ruth 1-4; James 1:27

QUESTION
What is most memorable to you about your conversations with
others?

I CAN'T EXPLAIN IT!
During summer break from school, Susan visited her relatives
in another city. They invited her to attend Sunday School and
worship with them. Susan was only 12 years old at the time;
her cousins were teenagers and they had attended church for
several years. Sunday School was fun, but Susan was more
interested in the worship service with the gospel singing,
fervent prayers, and preaching. When the pastor invited people
to join the church, Susan felt an overwhelming desire to go
forward.

Although she didn't understand what all this meant at the time,
Susan felt a love for Jesus she could not explain. The preacher
told her she would be baptized next month. Getting baptized
next month! But she had never seen a baptismal service. When
she returned to her seat, her cousins were so excited, and told
her she had made a good decision.

During the next few weeks, Susan had time to ponder and ask questions about what happens when you get baptized. Her family members assured her this would be a most wonderful experience.

On the evening of her baptism, Susan was dressed in white and waited with the others to be baptized. Although she was at peace about being baptized, she couldn't help wondering how she would feel afterward.

That evening when Susan returned home and everyone asked her if she felt any different, she honestly said, "I really don't feel different, but something has come over me that I cannot explain."

DISCUSSION
How did Susan's experiences at church and her discussions with her cousins lead her to accept Jesus into her heart and life?

TRANSITION
We see in this story that Susan accepted Christ by faith. God's amazing grace is extended to all who come to Him through faith. In this lesson, we learn that God's grace is extended to Naomi through her devoted daughter-in-law.

SCRIPTURE VOCABULARY
Entreat—to ask earnestly, beseech, implore
Blessed—favored, happy, joyful
Nourisher—one who helps sustain life and promotes growth

SCRIPTURE REFERENCE
Ruth 1:8-9, 16-18; 4:13-17
8 And Naomi said unto her two daughters in law, Go, return each to her mother's house: the LORD deal kindly with you, as ye have dealt with the dead, and with me.

9 The LORD grant you that ye may find rest, each of you in the house of her husband. Then she kissed them; and they lifted up their voice, and wept.

1:16 And Ruth said, Intreat me not to leave thee, or to return from following after thee: for whither thou goest, I will go; and where thou lodgest, I will lodge: thy people shall be my people, and thy God my God:

17 Where thou diest, will I die, and there will I be buried: the LORD do so to me, and more also, if ought but death part thee and me.

18 When she saw that she was stedfastly minded to go with her, then she left speaking unto her.

4:13 So Boaz took Ruth, and she was his wife: and when he went in unto her, the LORD gave her conception, and she bare a son.

14 And the women said unto Naomi, Blessed be the LORD, which hath not left thee this day without a kinsman, that his name may be famous in Israel.

15 And he shall be unto thee a restorer of thy life, and a nourisher of thine old age: for thy daughter in law, which loveth thee, which is better to thee than seven sons, hath born him.

16 And Naomi took the child, and laid it in her bosom, and became nurse unto it.

17 And the women her neighbours gave it a name, saying, There is a son born to Naomi; and they called his name Obed: he is the father of Jesse, the father of David.

MEMORY VERSE

"Beloved, let us love one another: for love is of God" (from 1 John 4:7).

HOW DOES THE MEMORY VERSE APPLY TO YOUR FAITH WALK?

_____

_____

_____

LESSON FOCUS

The main point of this lesson is to show the importance of loving-kindness in family relationships. In this case, a Jewish matriarch's faith in God was the spiritual linkage to her Moabite daughter-in-law's conversion to the God of the Hebrews.

BIBLE BACKGROUND

The book of Ruth is a short story how family relationships between a daughter-in-law who decides to leave her people and accept her mother-in-law's God, and about a near-relative who shows God's grace to Ruth and Naomi. The daughter-in-law finds favor in the sight of Naomi's near-relative and is rewarded for her loving-kindness. The story takes place during the time of the judges. Because of the "similarity of language of Ruth to that of Judges and Samuel," tradition accepted Samuel as the author of Ruth. The book must have been written at a later time because David is mentioned In Ruth 4:17. Some scholars date the book to the last third of the second millennium B.C.; that's "the period between the initial conquest of Palestine under Joshua and the establishment of the monarch under Saul" (*Expositors' Bible Commentary*, 1994, 368).

Family Relationships
Naomi's family ties are with the "Ephrathites of Bethlehem of Judah." She is also a near relative of Boaz. The "story of Ruth celebrates the family and the way it continues through generation" (www.womeninthebible, 12). The author of Ruth introduces the Deuteromic Law regarding levirate marriage into the plot when Boaz and Ruth plan to marry (Ruth 4:14). Levirate marriage gives the dead husband's nearest relative the rights to acquire all his land and his widow through marriage (Ruth 4:1-10). How would this work in your community or family?

The Community of Women
The women in Naomi's hometown welcome her back, and affirm that God has both blessed her with a devoted daughter-in-law and given her new life through the birth of a grandson. The "interpretative role of the community was essential for creating a new image of God's intention: redeeming the role of women and women's friendship in the language of story and song!" (Bankson, 1987, 129). God's purpose for Naomi's new life was expressed through the community of women.

SCRIPTURE EXPLORATION

> ***Ruth 1:8-9—And Naomi said unto her two daughters in law, Go return each to her mother's house: the LORD deal kindly with you, as ye have dealt with the dead, and with me. 9 The LORD grant you that ye may find rest, each of you in the house of her husband. Then she kissed them; and they lifted up their voice, and wept.***

Naomi started to return to Bethlehem with her two daughters-in-law, Orpah and Ruth, because she heard the famine was over, and the Lord had considered His people and blessed them with food. Naomi tries to convince her daughters-in-law to return to their mother's house, and she pronounces a blessing on them: "May the Lord deal kindly with you, as you have dealth with the dead and with me." Naomi continues her blessing and asks the Lord to grant that they may find "rest" or "security" in the house of their husband. Jewish women were completely dependent upon males to provide for their welfare. Because Naomi's husband and two sons were deceased, these women were widows without someone to care for them. Theirs was a friendship that lasted over a 10-year period (Ruth 1:4) and the thought of parting was difficult for the women.

Ruth 1:16-18—And Ruth said, Entreat me not to leave thee, or to return from following after thee: for whither thou goest, I will go; and where thou lodgest, I will lodge: thy people shall be my people, and thy God my God: 17 Where thou diest, will I die, and there will I be buried: the LORD do so to me, and more also, if ought but death part thee and me. 18 When she saw that she was stedfastly minded to go with her, then she left speaking unto her.

Although Orpah took Naomi's advice and returned to Moab, Ruth was not of the same mind. No doubt she made a decision to go with Naomi all the way to Bethlehem. So Ruth, whose name means "companion," becomes a "perfect example of Israelite faithfulness at its best" (*Reading the Old Testament*, 501). Ruth makes a wise choice and proclaims her constant love and devotion to Naomi, like Elisha to Elijah (2 Kings 2:2), and accepts Naomi's God as her God. Naomi realizes Ruth was steadfastly or determined to go along with her, so she stopped urging her to return to Moab.

Ruth 4:13-17—So Boaz took Ruth, and she was his wife: and when he went in unto her, the LORD gave her conception, and she bare a son. 14 And the women said unto Naomi, Blessed be the LORD, which hath not left thee this day without a kinsman, that his name may be famous in Israel. 5 And he shall be unto thee a restorer of thy life, and a nourisher of thine old age: for thy daughter in law, which loveth thee, which is better to thee than seven sons, hath born him. 16 And Naomi took the child, and laid it in her bosom, and became nurse unto it. 17 And the women her neighbours gave it a name, saying, There is a son born to Naomi; and they called his name Obed: he is the father of Jesse, the father of David.

Boaz became the instrument of the kindness to Ruth that Ruth showed to Naomi when he took her as his wife and became her redeemer kinsman (*Matthew Henry's Commentary in One Volume*, 280). The nearest kinsman could step in and buy back the property of his relative. Boaz was one of the nearest kinsman of Naomi's late husband, Elimelech, and his two sons. The kinsman became known as the "Goel," which means to "redeem" or "buy back" (http://www.abideinchrist. com). According to levirate marriage (Leviticus 25:48), the redeemer had to fulfill four requirements: (1) be the nearest kinsman (Leviticus 25:48); (2) be able to redeem; (3) be willing to redeem, and (4) be able to pay the price (Leviticus 25:27 and Ruth 4:7-11). Boaz fulfilled all the requirements and married Ruth.

The Lord enabled Ruth to conceive and give birth to a son. The townswomen pronounced a blessing on Naomi. They proclaimed that the baby born to Ruth would be famous throughout Israel, and he would renew Naomi's life and be a nourisher in her old age. According to Jewish custom, the firstborn son held a special place of honor within the family and was expected to take greater responsibility than his brothers (*Manners and Customs*, 414). Therefore, the women said to Naomi, "Your daughter-in-law who loves you is better to you than seven sons." Then Naomi took the baby and cared for him, and the women named the baby Obed. Parents of the child usually did the naming. "Often a name was given that referred to a personality trait the parents hoped would describe the child as he reached adulthood" (*Manners and Customs*, 446). Obed means "servant," and it was expected he would be the provider or the one to serve his grandmother, Naomi, in her old age.

DISCUSSION
1. What character traits do you admire in Naomi's relationship with her daughters-in-law?
2. In view of what you have learned about Ruth and her devotion to her mother-in-law, how can you enhance your relationship with the elders in your family—your mother, father, or grandparents?
3. How would you describe the pros and cons of the levirate marriage?
4. What is the significance of naming the firstborn in your family?
5. How important is it that the firstborn son is named after his father?

PRACTICAL APPLICATION
PERSONAL APPLICATION
Do you think it is important for grandparents to share their faith journey with their grandchildren? Describe how you have shared your faith with the younger generation. If you have not

done so before, think of a younger child to whom you can share your faith journey.

COMMUNITY APPLICATION

Speak with your pastor and worship leaders about planning an ecumenical worship service or with other faith communities. Create an opportunity after the services for persons to fellowship and ask questions regarding the worship services.

MEDITATION

As Christian believers, let us use every opportunity we have to share our faith with the next generation. Just as Naomi's faith had a positive influence on Ruth's decision to accept her God, we can also lead members of our families to our God. Throughout the summer, commit to showing loving-kindness to all family members. Note any positive feedback you receive from them. Then, make a commitment to share your faith with people you meet at your job. May our God continue to use you, through your Christian character and principles, to draw others to accept our Christ as their Lord and Savior.

PRAYER

Dear Heavenly Father, we thank You for the opportunities of sharing our faith journey with the next generation of believers. Father, we ask for Your forgiveness for the times we have not shared our faith with others. We ask for Your guidance and wisdom to know how to be more effective in sharing our faith with the next generation and beyond.

BIBLIOGRAPHY

Abide in Christ. Accessed September 16, 2012. http://www.abideinchrist.com.

Bankson, Marjory Zoet. *Seasons of Friendship*, 1987, 129.

Barker, Kenneth L., and John R. Kohlenberger III. *Expositor's Bible Commentary: Abridged Edition Old Testament,* 1994, 368.

Bible Gateway. Accessed August 28, 2012. http://www.biblegateway.com.

Boadt, Lawrence. *Reading the Old Testament*, 1984.

Hals, Ronald M. *The Theology of the Book of Ruth*, 1969, 16.

Henry, Matthew. *Matthew Henry's Commentary On the Whole Bible in One Volume*, 1960, 280.

Holy Bible, Original African Heritage Study Bible. King James Version, 1997.

Packer, J.I., and Tenney, M.C., eds. *Illustrated Manners and Customs of the Bible.* T. Nelson, 1980, 414, 446.

Women in the Bible. Accessed August 3, 2012. http://www.womeninthebible.com.

7

It Is Amazing!

LESSON SCRIPTURE
LUKE 2:41-52

BACKGROUND SCRIPTURES
Exodus 23:14-17; Matthew 13:55-56; Luke 2:35, 8:19;
John 7:1-10; Colossians 3:20; 1 Peter 2:13, 3:1, 5:5

QUESTION
What has amazed you about how God works in your life and
how He has answered your prayers?

IT'S AMAZING!

During the time of the Iraq War, many grandparents, aunts,
uncles, and other relatives became full-time guardians of their
family members' children when their sons and daughters were
deployed. Although guardianship was a new responsibility for
some, it was also a time for aunts, uncles to teach their nieces
and nephews to pray before bedtime each night. For one aunt,
guardianship involved two young toddlers since both mother
and father were serving in the Iraq War. Every night was a
special time of prayer because the children remembered how
much they missed Mommy and Daddy. So their prayer time
was usually a time of tears.

After several months of teaching her three-year-old nephew
to pray, one aunt was especially touched when the boy
awakened from his afternoon nap and came running in the

room, saying, "My daddy is coming home!" Since no one had told the boy his father would soon return home, it was truly an amazing statement. The boy's aunt asked, "How do you know your daddy is coming home?" He answered, "I just had a dream...my daddy's coming home!"

The aunt said she had tears of joy as she hugged her nephew and said to him, "God has answered our prayers." One month later, the boy's father returned home and two months later, his mother also came home safely. God answered the family's prayers and showed it to a three-year-old child in a dream. It's just amazing what God can do when you believe.

DISCUSSION
How important is it to you to spend time in prayer with your children or children in your family?

TRANSITION
Teaching our children to pray is a Christian duty. Children and youth, including toddlers, follow the examples we set for them.

SCRIPTURE VOCABULARY:
To Seek — to go in search of someone or something.
Wisdom — the power of right discernment.
Stature — the natural development of the human body.

SCRIPTURE REFERENCE
Luke 2:41-52
41 Now his parents went to Jerusalem every year at the feast of the passover.
42 And when he was twelve years old, they went up to Jerusalem after the custom of the feast.
43 And when they had fulfilled the days, as they returned,

the child Jesus tarried behind in Jerusalem; and Joseph and his mother knew not of it.

44 But they, supposing him to have been in the company, went a day's journey; and they sought him among their kinsfolk and acquaintance.

45 And when they found him not, they turned back again to Jerusalem, seeking him.

46 And it came to pass, that after three days they found him in the temple, sitting in the midst of the doctors, both hearing them, and asking them questions.

47 And all that heard him were astonished at his understanding and answers.

48 And when they saw him, they were amazed: and his mother said unto him, Son, why hast thou thus dealt with us? behold, thy father and I have sought thee sorrowing.

49 And he said unto them, How is it that ye sought me? wist ye not that I must be about my Father's business?

50 And they understood not the saying which he spake unto them.

51 And he went down with them, and came to Nazareth, and was subject unto them: but his mother kept all these sayings in her heart.

52 And Jesus increased in wisdom and stature, and in favour with God and man.

MEMORY VERSE

"Children, obey your parents in the Lord: for this is right." (Ephesians 6:1).

HOW DOES THE MEMORY VERSE APPLY TO YOUR FAITH WALK?

_____

_____

_____

LESSON FOCUS

The main focus of this lesson is to show that all who encountered the boy Jesus were amazed at His understanding and knowledge when they heard and saw Him in the temple.

BIBLE BACKGROUND

The gospel of Luke was written for a "predominantly gentile Christian community in a Greek speaking setting" (*Oxford Companion to the Bible*, 1993, 472). Most scholars generally agree the book was composed "after the fall of Jerusalem in 70 A.D." and is believed to have been written between 80 and 85 A.D. Luke's manuscript was directed to a Greek patron, Theophilus, with a two-fold purpose: (1) to present an orderly historical record of Jesus' ministry, and (2) to present an apologetic for the Christian faith to show that Christianity posed no political threat" (*Holman Illustrated Bible Dictionary*, 2003, 1058). Of the four gospel writers, Luke is the only one who provides some details about Jesus' early childhood life, showing His wisdom beyond the formative years. The boy Jesus was 12 years old at the time the family journeyed to Jerusalem to celebrate Passover. At 12 years of age, a Jewish boy "became a son of the law and began to observe the ordinances" (*Word Pictures in the New Testament*, 2000, 116).

The Passover Festival in the Temple at Jerusalem

God established Passover as one of the festivals Jewish people celebrated as an observance of Israel's liberation from Egyptian bondage (Exodus 12:1–27, 23:15; Numbers 9:2–14). Jesus' family were devout Jews, and they journeyed to Jerusalem every year to celebrate Passover (Luke 2:41). These holy convocations were for appointed times and places (Leviticus 23:1–7; Deuteronomy 16:1–8). Passover, the first of three annual festivals, took place on the 14th day of the first month at twilight; it was also called the Feast of Unleavened Bread because only unleavened bread (Exodus 23:15) was eaten during the seven days immediately following Passover (*Holman Illustrated Bible Dictionary*, 2003, 567-568). The temple at Jerusalem is where Israel's people met to celebrate Passover. This is where the boy Jesus encounters teachers and lawyers in the temple and amazes them with His understanding and intelligence beyond His formative years (Luke 2:46–47).

SCRIPTURE EXPLORATION

Luke 2:41-47—Now his parents went to Jerusalem every year at the feast of the passover. 42 And when he was twelve years old, they went up to Jerusalem after the custom of the feast. 43 And when they had fulfilled the days, as they returned, the child Jesus tarried behind in Jerusalem; and Joseph and his mother knew not of it. 44 But they, supposing him to have been in the company, went a day's journey; and they sought him among their kinsfolk and acquaintance. 45 And when they found him not, they turned back again to Jerusalem, seeking him. 46 And it came to pass, that after three days they found him in the temple, sitting in the midst of the doctors, both hearing them, and asking them questions. 47 And all that heard him were astonished at his understanding and answers.

Jesus' parents were devout Jewish people and they went to Jerusalem to commemorate Passover (Pesach)—God's deliverance of the Israelites out of slavery. The Jewish people were to remember always what God had done for them (Exodus 6:7 and Numbers 15:41). After the festival was over, Jesus stayed behind at the temple, but Joseph and Mary were unaware they had left Him. At the age of 12, Jesus might have been with the women and children, or with the men and older boys. This was the way families grouped together (*Expositors Bible Commentary New Testament*, 220). After searching for Him among family members and friends, Mary and Joseph turned back to Jerusalem. After three days, they found Him in the temple. The temple is where Israel's teachers of the law encounter the boy Jesus. He demonstrates superior understanding and ability of the law, though He is too young to have gained this kind of knowledge from formal training (*Harper Collins Study Bible*, NRSV, 1766). The 12-year-old Jesus amazes all who hear Him.

Luke 2:48-50—And when they saw him, they were amazed: and his mother said unto him, Son, why hast thou thus dealt with us? behold, thy father and I have sought thee sorrowing. 49 And he said unto them, How is it that ye sought me? wist ye not that I must be about my Father's business? 50 And they understood not the saying which he spake unto them.

When Mary and Joseph found Jesus, Mary asks Jesus why He dealt with them in this way; they were seeking Him and sorrowful about His disappearance from the group. Mary's questions demonstrate the deep emotional feeling parents have for a missing child. But Jesus asks her, "Why were you looking for me? Didn't you know that I had to be here, dealing with the things of my Father?" (*Message Bible*). Jesus' response and questions shows His mission (John 9:4) and the first implication of Himself as the Son of the Father. His parents did not understand what He was talking about.

Luke 2:51-52—51 And he went down with them, and came to Nazareth, and was subject unto them: but his mother kept all these sayings in her heart. 52 And Jesus increased in wisdom and stature, and in favour with God and man.

Jesus modeled behavior of children toward their parents as He was obedient to His earthly parents, according to Exodus 20:12. Jesus shows perfect humanity by His human behavior. Although Jesus' growth in stature was entirely normal, His growth in wisdom does not detract from His deity. Luke's description of Jesus were the words used to describe Samuel when he was a boy (1 Samuel 2:26).

DISCUSSION
What lessons can we learn from Mary and Joseph, who assumed Jesus was with them when they'd actually left Him in the temple? What does "turning back" to Jerusalem tell us about our spiritual journey? Does this lesson give you encouragement of where to look if you are out of fellowship with a church family? Does this lesson encourage you to have more zeal in your ministry and service? Jesus was obedient to His earthly parents. What are your attitudes about teaching children obedience to their parents and those in authority?

PRACTICAL APPLICATION
PERSONAL APPLICATION
Do you have a time for weekly prayer with family or friends? Why not start a weekly telephone prayer conference call with senior citizens who may be shut-ins? Or, start a group with parents who have small children at home and cannot get out for weekly prayer meeting? Think of military families who attend your church and have irregular work hours or varying travel and duty schedules. Maybe the participants could suggest the best time to join in a conference call.

COMMUNITY APPLICATION

Jesus spent time in the temple listening to and asking questions of the doctors. Think of some places you could spend time listening to and asking questions of teenagers who need guidance and mentoring. If you are single, do you have teenage family members with whom you could mentor? Are there any coworkers, sorority sisters, fraternity brothers, or church friends who have teenagers you could mentor?

MEDITATION

Luke reports on the boy Jesus in the temple listening to the doctors and rabbis. As disciples of Christ, we endeavor to grow spiritually by engaging our ministers and teachers. Although we cannot ask questions during a sermon, we can engage our Sunday School and Bible teachers. Church attendance on Sunday is another time to celebrate our Lord's resurrection and to listen to God's message. Jesus showed by His example that we should not only listen to our teachers, but be in dialogue with them as well.

PRAYER

Dear Heavenly Father, we thank You for the opportunity to learn more about Your Son, who has shown us how to follow You. We ask for Your forgiveness for the times we have not obeyed Your Word. And we seek Your wisdom and knowledge to guide us on our spiritual journey. In Jesus' name we pray, amen.

BIBLIOGRAPHY

Barker, Kenneth L., and John R. Kohlenberger III. *Expositor's Bible Commentary New Testament*, 1994.
Bible Gateway. Accessed August 28, 2012. http://www.biblegateway.com/.
Holman Illustrated Bible Dictionary, 2003, 567-568, 1058.
Meeks, Wayne A., ed. *Harper Collins Study Bible*, NRSV, 1989, 1766.
Oxford Companion to the Bible, 1993, 472.
Word Pictures in the New Testament, 2000, 116.

8

A Family Affair

LESSON SCRIPTURE
1 SAMUEL 1:10-20

BACKGROUND SCRIPTURES
Genesis 30:2, 22; 33:5; Numbers 6:1–21; Judges 13; 1 Samuel 1–2; Psalm 127:3; Matthew 19:4–6; 1 Peter 5:7

QUESTION
The family is the basic unit of God's kingdom and prays together as a spiritual unit. We all come from a family. Share how you are part of a spiritual family. Why is this important to you and for the body of Christ? It is the desire of Jesus Christ that we be one spiritual family of believers, whose focus is on God.

BENT BUT NOT BROKEN
Wilma Rudolph was a great American athlete who defied the odds to achieve success. She was born prematurely—weighing 4 ½ pounds—and reared in St. Bethlehem, Tennessee, located 45 miles southeast of Nashville.

Wilma was born into a blended family of 19 brothers and sisters. It was a large and loving family. Her father worked as a railroad porter and her mother performed domestic work, cleaning houses six days a week. Wilma contracted polio at age four, which eventually led to the inability to use her left leg. For the next five years, Wilma received daily leg massages from her siblings, since her parents had to work. She walked with braces until she was nine years old.

Can you imagine the ridicule Wilma, with her legs in braces, might have endured from her classmates? She could have been bitter toward her physicians, who believed she would never walk. Perhaps we might think that God has done us a disservice by placing challenges before us.

A praying family who loves God expects miracles to happen. Wilma regained strength in her left leg, began running, and never lost a track meet during her high school career. At age 16, she won a bronze medal in the Summer Olympics in Melbourne, Australia. At the 1960 Olympics, Wilma became the first American woman to win three gold medals in the track and field competition.

DISCUSSION
Have you overcome great odds in your personal, spiritual, financial, political, or social life? Can you provide examples of the difficult times you have overcome with the aid of God? What has God given us that permits us to survive, even when faced with insurmountable odds?

TRANSITION
Our lesson encourages us to pray for others to persevere, even when the circumstances may seem impossible. Although we may face public rejection, humiliation, and ridicule, praying through our difficulties is most important to being a true disciple of God.

SCRIPTURE VOCABULARY
Officers — Administrators of the king. The word is the same term for *eunuch*, however, it is most likely to mean officers in this instance.

Confectionaries — People who make perfume or mix

ointments used for anointing.

Ear his ground — To do the plowing and harvesting of the crops.

Chariot — A light, open, two-wheeled vehicle pulled by one or more horses.

SCRIPTURE REFERENCE

1 Samuel 8:10–20

10 And Samuel told all the words of the LORD unto the people that asked of him a king.

11 And he said, This will be the manner of the king that shall reign over you: He will take your sons, and appoint them for himself, for his chariots, and to be his horsemen; and some shall run before his chariots.

12 And he will appoint him captains over thousands, and captains over fifties; and will set them to ear his ground, and to reap his harvest, and to make his instruments of war, and instruments of his chariots.

13 And he will take your daughters to be confectionaries, and to be cooks, and to be bakers.

14 And he will take your fields, and your vineyards, and your oliveyards, even the best of them, and give them to his servants.

15 And he will take the tenth of your seed, and of your vineyards, and give to his officers, and to his servants.

16 And he will take your menservants, and your maidservants, and your goodliest young men, and your asses, and put them to his work.

17 He will take the tenth of your sheep: and ye shall be his servants.

18 And ye shall cry out in that day because of your king which ye shall have chosen you; and the LORD will not hear you in that day.

19 Nevertheless the people refused to obey the voice of Samuel; and they said, Nay; but we will have a king over us;

20 That we also may be like all the nations; and that our king may judge us, and go out before us, and fight our battles.

MEMORY VERSE

"The effectual fervent prayer of a righteous man availeth much" (from James 5:16).

HOW DOES THE MEMORY VERSE APPLY TO YOUR FAITH WALK?

_____

_____

_____

LESSON FOCUS

The main idea of this lesson is that praying for others is important, especially when difficulties and challenges cause hardship for ourselves and our families. In walking with God, praying for others is always appropriate.

BIBLE BACKGROUND

Samuel was an extraordinary man who served in multiple capacities as a priest, prophet, and Israel's last judge (*Richards*, 1987, S.199). Samuel served as a judge in Israel shortly before 1051 B.C. In our text, Samuel was approximately 65 to 70 years old (*Willmington*, 1999, S. 1 Samuel 8:10–18). Many in Israel, particularly the elders of the community, believed Samuel's leadership suffered because of his age. Additionally, the appointment of Samuel's two sons as judges in Beersheba, 50 miles south of Ramah, added fuel to the growing debate concerning Samuel's leadership. Joel and Abijah (vv. 1-5) were corrupt, despicable, and dishonest judges who probably reminded the people of Eli's wicked sons (*Willmington*, 1999, S. 1 Samuel 8:10–18). As a result, the children of Israel demanded a king. Samuel believed the people were rejecting his leadership. Although they were opposing his leadership, God reminded Samuel that the people were really rejecting Him. It appears the people were rejecting both God and Samuel. Samuel was instructed to share with the people that their desire for a king would be granted. Their choice of a king would leave their country in ruins and force their children to become virtual slaves to the king.

SCRIPTURE EXPLORATION

Israel is shifting its focus from a godly, theocratic religious belief system to a more secular and worldly view, similar to that of its neighbors. Surrounding nations were led by secular military kingships that Israel envied. Israel had always struggled with following God, the directives of God, or the representatives of God. At various times in its history, Israel showed movement away from God rather than toward God. Turning away from God displeases Him and, in most cases, ends negatively for the people. In each case, any distancing from God seems to exacerbate the community's hardships.

When there is separation from God, He will not only destroy the wicked but also the righteous (Genesis 18:23–30). When Sodom and Gomorrah were destroyed, Abraham could not find 10 righteous men in the city. In the end, not only did God destroy both cities, but Lot lost his wife because she did not adhere to the Godly advice that might have saved her life. Instead, Lot's wife finds her burial ground in a pillar of salt.

Not adhering to the mandate of God can lead to dire—and sometimes fatal—consequences. For example, Moses followed God's directive by returning to Egypt to liberate the

Hebrews from bondage. The people wanted to stone Moses to death because they believed leaving Egypt was a mistake. This is why the people spoke against God—believing Moses had brought them out of Egypt only to die of starvation in the wilderness. God was well-aware of their circumstances and, as a result of their complaint, many died when God sent fiery serpents among the people to bite them (Judges 21:5).

Additionally, while Moses received the Ten Commandments at Mount Sinai, the people requested that Aaron make them gods, so he fashioned a golden calf (Deuteronomy 32:1–6). The second commandment explicitly prohibits idolatry: "Thou shall not have any graven images" (Deuteronomy 20:4). Moses faced tremendous difficulties, not only having to deal with Israel worshipping an idol god, but also his own biological brother leading this spiritual rebellion. Finally, Baal worship was common during the times of the monarchy (Beitzel and Elwell, 1988, S. 1014). To seek a king as a lord is flirting with idolatry. The thirst to taste what it meant to serve other gods, even when it was to the detriment of Israel, shows the depth of their spiritual decline.

A common thread throughout this discussion is Israel's willingness to depart from following God, the directives of God, or the representatives of God. We discover Israel was slowly moving toward a secularized worldview, similar to its neighbors. The movement toward a monarchy rather than maintaining a theocracy alerts us to the earthly, physical and non-spiritual outlook of Israel. Rather than walking by faith, which is a spiritual and Godly posture, its residents are walking by sight, which is a worldly view.

Representatives of God always seem to encounter people who question their ascent to leadership by the hand of God. The path to leadership is never a pretty sight nor one without tribulation. The Bible is replete with instances of the conflict between spokesmen for God and the people God sent to be led by Him.

The desire for a king who will rule over them becomes paramount in Israel's quest to emulate the surrounding nations. This movement from theocracy to monarchy is a critical shift in the life of the community, fraught with unseen challenges and danger. Samuel the prophet provides the clarion call of caution and warnings about this new king.

The king who shall rule over them can be described in the following manner:

Relation to Labor: verses 11–13, 16
These Scriptures deal with the various classes of exploited labor in Israel. In each instance, Israel's sons and daughters are required to work for the king, which is forced labor. Military conscription is the rule rather than an exception. Females are designated as domesticated kitchen help, working as cooks and bakers. Additionally, womens' primary duties are as mixers of ointment that can be manufactured into perfume.

Relation to the Land: verses 14–15, 17
To control the land is the basis for wealth and civic, political, and earthly power. The king will force the children of Israel to farm the land. The king's regime seizes land and real property, to be divided among his servants. Ten percent of the vineyard and olive yards will be given to select officials of the king's cabinet. It is possible but unlikely that these officials could be eunuchs because the Hebrew word is the same in both instances. Because of the context of the word usage, however, it probably refers to officials rather that eunuchs.

Decision Time: verses 18–20

There are two important decisions here. The first decision is that the time will come when the children of Israel will call upon God and God will refuse to listen to their request. Second, it was the people's refusal to heed to Samuel and still desire a king; God finally grants Israel's request for a king.

PRACTICAL APPLICATION
PERSONAL APPLICATION
1. Take a moment to write down any personal difficulties or challenges—past or present—you've faced in your life.

_____

_____

_____

_____

2. How would you advise others on integrity in leadership?

_____

_____

_____

COMMUNITY APPLICATION
1. You are a participant in Samuel's community. Discuss ways to unify the community in light of its dissatisfaction with leadership.

_____

_____

_____

2. Do you believe godly parents can influence their children? Do godly parents always produce godly children? Express your thoughts in writing and discuss with the class what the church can implement to help.

_____

_____

_____

_____

_____

MEDITATION

Prayer is always appropriate when bringing family members together in times of joy and pain. It is a conversation, a discussion, or a dialogue about life. We discuss with God the plethora of what this life offers and what the next life holds. Personal tragedy and challenges are common occurrences in the human experience. Samuel was obviously hurt because of the sins of his sons, as well as being rejected by a community in which he served for such a long time. Such painful experiences force us to look to God. Our families feel the brunt of the pain our loved ones may endure while battling life's circumstances. Yet, those of us who see life through spiritual lenses realize that praying people are better able to withstand the difficult days because of an unshakable faith in God. Prayer does change things, circumstances, and lives.

PRAYER

God of peace and love, grant us the wisdom to make the right decisions, even in disappointing circumstances. We need stronger families and request You provide us with Your divine protection. O Lord, we ask these prayers to You as our Father. You sent Jesus to allow us to see an example of earthly suffering and heavenly victory. We ask this in Jesus' name, amen.

REFERENCES

African American Quotes. "Wilma Rudolph." Accessed August 22, 2012. http://african American quotes.org//wilma-rudolph.html

Beitzel, Barry J., and Elwell, Walter A. Baker Encyclopedia of the Bible. Grand Rapids, MI: Baker Book House, 1988, S. 1014.

Bible Gateway. "1 Samuel 8:10–20 (King James Version). Accessed Aug. 22, 2012. http://www.biblegateway.com/passage/?search=1%20Samuel%208:10-20&version=KJV

Jennings, F. Dake's Annotated Reference Bible. Lawrenceville, GA: Dake Bible Sales, Inc., 1988.

Jewish Publication Society. The Jewish Study Bible. Edited by Adele Berlin and Marc Zvi Brettler. New York, NY: Oxford University Press, 1985, 1999.

Noteable Biographies. "Brothers and Sisters." Accessed August 22, 2012. www.notablebiographies.com/Ro-Sc/Rudolph-Wilma.html

Omanson, Roger L., and Ellington, John. A Handbook on the First Book of Samuel. New York, NY: United Bible Societies, 2001 (UBS Handbook Series), S.164.

Richards, Larry. The Teachers Commentary. Wheaton, IL: Victor Books, 1987, S. 199.

Willmington, H.L. The Outline Bible. Wheaton, IL: Tyndale House Publishers, 1999, S. 1 Sa 8:10–18.

9

Astonishing Growth!

―――――――

LESSON SCRIPTURE
ACTS 2:38–47

BACKGROUND SCRIPTURES
Acts 1:14; 2:21, 46; 6:4; 8:13; 10:7; Romans 12:12; 13:6;
Colossians 4:2

QUESTION
Describe a time when you shared your faith with someone
who was not saved. How did you feel? Did the conversation
give the person a desire to come to Christ?

EVANGELISM JITTERS
Brian was nervous about going door-to-door for Saturday morning
evangelism. The entire congregation had been invited to join the
Evangelism Ministry team and go into the community to share the
Gospel. Brian prayed that morning before leaving the house, but
as he drove into the church's parking lot, his palms were sweaty
and his hands were shaking.

   Joe approached Brian's car and tapped on the window. "Hey,
man!" Joe said, smiling.

   A little startled, Brian smiled and said, "Hey."

   Brian opened the car door and extended his hand to shake
Joe's. Joe gave him a firm handshake, and asked, "Are you
ready?"

   "Not really," Brian exhaled. "I can't believe I'm this nervous.
I've never evangelized publicly before."

"Yes you have," Joe replied. "It may not have been door-to-door, but you share the gospel more than anyone else I know. The church is full of your family, friends, and co-workers because you always share your faith and invite people to visit our church."

"Wow, I guess I never thought about it like that," Brian said. "Thanks, that makes me feel so much more at ease! I'll just do what I always do, and trust God to do the rest."

DISCUSSION
Why do you think Brian was so nervous about going out to publicly evangelize when, in fact, he was already used to sharing the gospel with his family members and co-workers?

TRANSITION
In today's story, Brian was very nervous about sharing his faith with strangers. He didn't realize he shared his faith on a regular basis with his family and co-workers. In the Scripture text, we not only see 3,000 souls being saved in one day, but also see God adding souls to the church daily. In today's lesson, we are reminded that our responsibility is to share our faith with others and then let God do the rest.

SCRIPTURE VOCABULARY
Baptized — A religious sacrament marked by the symbolic application of water to the head or immersion of the body into water, resulting in admission of the recipient into the community of Christians.

Testify — To make a statement based on personal knowledge in support of an asserted fact; to bear witness.

Exhort — To encourage and strengthen by consolation; to comfort.

Doctrine — A rule or principle of law, especially when established by precedent.

SCRIPTURE REFERENCE

Acts 2:38-47

38 Then Peter said unto them, Repent, and be baptized every one of you in the name of Jesus Christ for the remission of sins, and ye shall receive the gift of the Holy Ghost.

39 For the promise is unto you, and to your children, and to all that are afar off, even as many as the Lord our God shall call.

40 And with many other words did he testify and exhort, saying, Save yourselves from this untoward generation.

41 Then they that gladly received his word were baptized: and the same day there were added unto them about three thousand souls.

42 And they continued stedfastly in the apostles' doctrine and fellowship, and in breaking of bread, and in prayers.

43 And fear came upon every soul: and many wonders and signs were done by the apostles.

44 And all that believed were together, and had all things common;

45 And sold their possessions and goods, and parted them to all men, as every man had need.

46 And they, continuing daily with one accord in the temple, and breaking bread from house to house, did eat their meat with gladness and singleness of heart,

47 Praising God, and having favour with all the people. And the Lord added to the church daily such as should be saved.

MEMORY VERSE

"Ye shall be witnesses unto me … unto the uttermost part of the earth" (from Acts 1:8).

HOW DOES THE MEMORY VERSE APPLY TO YOUR FAITH WALK?

_____

_____

_____

LESSON FOCUS

The objective of this lesson is to impress upon believers how important it is for Christians to not only witness to their family members, but to be prepared to do so by developing an action plan and leaning on the Holy Spirit for the empowerment to be effective.

BIBLE BACKGROUND

The book of Acts was written between 63 and 70 A.D. Luke wrote the book of Acts to give an account of the birth and growth of the Christian church. In Chapter One of Acts, Jesus promised the gift of the Holy Spirit to the disciples.

We learn in Chapter Two that on the day of Pentecost, the promised Holy Spirit arrived. Pentecost was originally an Old Testament festival. It was the second of the three great annual pilgrimage festivals during which many would go to the temple in Jerusalem. Pentecost (which literally means the 50th day) was celebrated on the Sabbath, the 50th day after the Passover celebration. In the Old Testament, Pentecost was also called the "Feast of First Fruits" and the "Feast of Harvest." Pentecost was celebrated the seventh week after Passover in grateful recognition of the completed harvest.

It was this annual feast that brought together Jewish people from 15 surrounding nations together. By the power of the

Holy Spirit, they each heard the Word of God in their native tongues (Acts 2:8–11). It was on this day that Peter preached to Jewish people from every nation, and about 3,000 non-believers were saved.

SCRIPTURE EXPLORATION

Acts 2:38–40—Then Peter said unto them, Repent, and be baptized every one of you in the name of Jesus Christ for the remission of sins, and ye shall receive the gift of the Holy Ghost. 39 For the promise is unto you, and to your children, and to all that are afar off, even as many as the Lord our God shall call. 40 And with many other words did he testify and exhort, saying, Save yourselves from this untoward generation.

The Day of Pentecost is the first time we see Peter after he is filled with the Holy Spirit. We have already seen glimpses of the very vocal Peter's personality and his ministry in the Gospels. More often than not, he ended up with his foot in his mouth. It was Peter who rebuked Jesus when Jesus told His disciples that He must suffer and die (Matthew 16:21–23). It was Peter who sliced off Malchus' ear in the garden (John 18:10–11). It was Peter who swore vehemently that he would never deny Christ (Mark 14:29–30). And yes, it was Peter who denied Christ three times before the cock crowed twice (Luke 22:60–61).

Despite all this, the Bible records a Spirit-filled Peter. On the Day of Pentecost, Peter stood to correct the accusations from the crowd that those who were speaking in unknown languages were drunk. He began his sermon quoting the prophet Joel (Joel 2:28–32), and ended some time later with 3,000 souls being converted.

Jesus had given instructions for His disciples to stay in

Jerusalem and wait for the Holy Spirit to come and fill them with power. Jesus also told His disciples that they were His witnesses and, beginning in Jerusalem, "repentance and remission of sins should be preached in his name among all nations" (from Luke 24:47). In this passage of Scripture, we discover Peter fulfilling his divine mandate.

> *Acts 2:41–47—Then they that gladly received his word were baptized: and the same day there were added unto them about three thousand souls. 42 And they continued stedfastly in the apostles' doctrine and fellowship, and in breaking of bread, and in prayers. 43 And fear came upon every soul: and many wonders and signs were done by the apostles. 44 And all that believed were together, and had all things common; 45 And sold their possessions and goods, and parted them to all men, as every man had need. 46 And they, continuing daily with one accord in the temple, and breaking bread from house to house, did eat their meat with gladness and singleness of heart, 47 Praising God, and having favour with all the people. And the Lord added to the church daily such as should be saved.*

In this Scripture passage, we get a bird's eye view of the fruit of the Holy Ghost, who is the Life-Giving Spirit. Jesus declared to His disciples during His earthly ministry that He did not come to abolish the Law, but to fulfill it instead (Matthew 5:17). When He was taken up, He told His disciples to wait in Jerusalem for the promised Holy Spirit to come. The Law brought forth death (1 Corinthians 15:56), but Jesus, the fulfillment of the Law, brought forth life. On the day Moses brought the Law—the 10 Commandments—down from Mt. Sinai, the Israelites had already proven they could not keep the laws, and the Law brought forth death. The day the Law was given, 3,000 people died (Exodus 32:28). The day the promised Holy Spirit came, 3,000 souls were given eternal life.

The Bible teaches us that where there is the Spirit of the Lord, there is liberty (2 Corinthians 3:17). We see the manifestation of the presence of God through the person of the Holy Spirit in the early church, not only through the signs and wonders performed by the disciples, but also through the unity of the believers.

On the night in which Jesus would be betrayed, He prayed. He prayed that God's children would experience such perfect unity that the world would know God sent Jesus, and that God loves His children as much as He loves Jesus (John 17:23). This passage of Scripture highlights the oneness Jesus prayed for. All believers were on one accord. They sold their possessions and there was no selfishness; therefore, there was no lack among them. They continued to worship together daily in the temple and eat together, going from one home to another. It was in this Spirit-filled atmosphere that God continued to add to His church by saving souls every day.

DISCUSSION

1. When the Jewish people in Jerusalem heard Peter's words, they were convicted, and asked him what they should do. What were Peter's instructions to them?
2. For whom was the promise of the Holy Spirit meant?
3. According to verse 42, to what four things did the new converts devote themselves?
4. What indicated that there existed a deep sense of unity among the believers in the early church?
5. Name at least two ways witnessing to your family can grow today's church.

6. How can you use the unity seen in the early church as a way to motivate yourself and others to share your faith with relatives and friends who are not saved?

PRACTICAL APPLICATION
PERSONAL APPLICATION

1. Fold a piece of paper in half two times to form a little booklet. This will be a tract when you finish. Take a few moments to think about your family members, and what might be the best theme to reach them. The tract doesn't have to be perfect. Write words of encouragement to invite someone to know Christ. Try to be creative. Remember to include the salvation plan on the inside of the tract (Romans 3:10, 3:23, 5:8, 6:23, 10:9-10).

2. Make a list of your family members (immediate and extended). Put a check by those family members you know are saved. Circle all the names of relatives who are not saved; also circle the names of any family members of whom you are unsure. Write 2 Peter 3:9 and 1 John 5:14–15 at the top of the paper. Take a few minutes to read those verses and pray for every circled name, asking God to save your loved ones and use you as a witness to lead them to salvation.

COMMUNITY APPLICATION

1. Pick an evening to host a family get-together. It can be a dinner, game night, or even a movie night. Try to have it in your home or someplace where there can be some intimacy—not a public arena, like a concert hall. Attempt to have as many relatives participate as possible. Have everyone bring his or her favorite dish, game, or movie. Spend time praying before the event takes place, and

ask God to make the evening a great time of fellowship. Also, ask God to lead you to ways you can incorporate Him into the evening without making your guests feel like they are attending a church service.

2. Suggest to your church leadership—and even help plan—a Sunday event specifically designated as "Family Day." Ask every member of the congregation to invite their entire family, immediate and extended, to church this particular Sunday. There can be a barbeque afterward, as well as a photographer on-hand to take family portraits. Consider offering a prize for the church member who brings the most visitors. You may invite your saved family members as well but this will be a great opportunity to invite your family members who are not saved. Consider making formal invitations, as you would for any event, and mail them to your family.

MEDITATION

Most believers understand the fundamental importance of sharing their faith, but many neglect to do it. Often, Christians don't share their faith with others—whether they are family members or strangers—because they are either afraid of being rejected or just nervous they won't know what to say. In today's Scripture, we read about the vital importance of sharing the gospel and the miraculous results when we allow the Holy Spirit to use us to do so.

Peter preached on the day of Pentecost and 3,000 souls were saved. That amount seems staggering to the average believer, but it is not one we have to reach. If we pray, trust God, and be bold enough to witness to our families, that alone will grow the church. It is not God's will that anyone should perish (2 Peter 3:9). Don't focus on trying to win 3,000 souls; focus on winning one soul at a time. Pray for your family members and ask God to show you the one to target for Christ. When that one is saved, choose one more. Before you know it, you will see the fruit of how witnessing grows the church!

PRAYER

Dear Heavenly Father, I pray for all my relatives who are not saved. Please give me the courage and boldness to witness to my family members. I pray You use me to grow Your church. Help me to witness— not just with my lips, but also with my life. I pray that my family will see my good works and give You glory. In Jesus' name, amen.

BIBLIOGRAPHY

Beth Anderson, Benjamin Fortson, Catherine Pratt and Hanna Schonthal, The American Heritage Dictionary of the English Language, 4th ed. (Boston: Houghton Mifflin, 2006), 142, 530, 1788.

Blue Letter Bible. "Dictionary and Word Search for parakaleō (Strong's 3870)". Blue Letter Bible. 1996-2012. http://www.blueletterbible.org/lang/lexicon/lexicon.cfm?Strongs=G3870&t=KJV (accessed 16 August 2012).

Blue Letter Bible. "Gospel of Luke 24 - (KJV - King James Version)." Blue Letter Bible. 1996-2012. http://www.blueletterbible.org/Bible.cfm?b=Luk&c=24&t=KJV (accessed 27 August 2012).

Blue Letter Bible. "Gospel of Matthew 4 - (KJV - King James Version)." Blue Letter Bible. 1996–2012. http://www.blueletterbible.org/Bible.cfm?b=Mat&c=4&t=KJV (accessed 28 August 2012).

Blue Letter Bible. "Acts of the Apostles 2 - (KJV - King James Version)." Blue Letter Bible. 1996-2012. http://www.blueletterbible.org/Bible.cfm?b=Act&c=2&t=KJV (accessed 28 August 2012).

Blue Letter Bible. "Paul's Epistle - Romans 12 - (NIV - New International Version)." Blue Letter Bible. 1996-2012. http://www.blueletterbible.org/Bible.cfm?b=Rom&c=12&t=NIV (accessed 28 August 2012).

Henry, Matthew. "Commentary on Acts 2." Blue Letter Bible. 2012. http:// www.blueletterbible.org/commentaries/comm_view.cfm?AuthorID=4&contentID=1690&commInfo=5&topic=Acts (accessed 29 August 2012).

Henry, Matthew. "Commentary on Acts 2." . Blue Letter Bible. 1 Mar 1996. 2012. http://www.blueletterbible.org/commentaries/ comm_view.cfm?AuthorID=4&contentID=1690&commInfo=5&topic=Acts (accessed 29 August 2012).

10

God Gives Us A Fresh Start

LESSON SCRIPTURE
REVELATION 21:1–7; 22:3–5

BACKGROUND SCRIPTURES:
Isaiah 65:17; 66:22; John 14:2; 1 Corinthians 15:52;
2 Peter 3:10–13

QUESTION
Describe a time when you experienced a fresh start on something that you loved and worked hard for, but in the end, the situation did not work out well. What thoughts and emotions filled you as you began anew with the blessing of a fresh start?

CELEBRATING NEW BEGINNINGS
Within days of celebrating college graduation, Randy entered military service. Rigorous basic training was immediately followed by survival training. At the end of survival training, he became a war captive. He was marched off to a prison camp, where he suffered through the experience of living as a prisoner of war. Randy was kept in a small cage or sometimes with fellow prisoners in a dark, dirty cell. On the third morning of imprisonment, they were all blindfolded, marched outdoors before dawn, and forced to stand at attention. For two hours, they listened to a man with a foreign accent talk about the many wrongs of their country. Randy stood there, yearning to return to the country the man decried. He missed his mother's

delicious cooking, talks with his father, his warm, clean bed, and having fun with his sisters, brothers, and friends. The man ended his speech by telling Randy and his fellow prisoners to turn around and remain still. For five minutes, there was complete silence. Then suddenly, a strong American voice said, "Take off your blindfolds, men. You are going home." Randy removed his blindfold and felt the searing pain of the morning sun in his eyes. His pain quickly fled, swallowed by the collective, joyous shouts of his fellow prisoners at seeing the American flag facing them atop a flagpole. The time of captivity was over. The time of freedom returned. Hallelujah!

DISCUSSION

Our lives are filled with many different beginnings and endings. It's possible for these occasions to become opportunities for celebration. Are there elements of college or military training that are similar or helpful to a Christian's preparation for service unto the Lord that give cause for celebration?

TRANSITION

We see in our story how new beginnings can spark celebrations that help fuel continued activity on the part of the celebrant. In this lesson, we find God's promise and its fulfillment in a new beginning for both heaven and earth, empowering life now and through eternity.

SCRIPTURE VOCABULARY

New Heaven and New Earth — a description of God's new creation, restoration, and renewal of all things in heaven and earth.

Light — symbolizes divine understanding and consciousness, the expansion of human awareness with truth.

Holy City, New Jerusalem — symbolizes the home of the saved, the inheritance of the saints, or the prepared place of the blessed.

Water of Life — the Spirit of God; the life that flows from God through a relationship with Christ Jesus.

SCRIPTURE REFERENCE

Revelation 21:1–7, 22:3-5

21:1 And I saw a new heaven and a new earth: for the first heaven and the first earth were passed away; and there was no more sea.

2 And I John saw the holy city, new Jerusalem, coming down from God out of heaven, prepared as a bride adorned for her husband.

3 And I heard a great voice out of heaven saying, Behold, the tabernacle of God is with men, and he will dwell with them, and they shall be his people, and God himself shall be with them, and be their God.

4 And God shall wipe away all tears from their eyes; and there shall be no more death, neither sorrow, nor crying, neither shall there be any more pain: for the former things are passed away.

5 And he that sat upon the throne said, Behold, I make all things new. And he said unto me, Write: for these words are true and faithful.

6 And he said unto me, It is done. I am Alpha and Omega, the beginning and the end. I will give unto him that is athirst of the fountain of the water of life freely.

7 He that overcometh shall inherit all things; and I will be his God, and he shall be my son.

22:3 And there shall be no more curse: but the throne of God and of the Lamb shall be in it; and his servants shall serve him:

4 And they shall see his face; and his name shall be in their foreheads.

5 And there shall be no night there; and they need no candle, neither light of the sun; for the Lord God giveth them light: and they shall reign for ever and ever.

MEMORY VERSE
"Rejoice, because your names are written in heaven" (from Luke 10:20).

HOW DOES THE MEMORY VERSE APPLY TO YOUR FAITH WALK?

_____

_____

_____

_____

LESSON FOCUS
God is a Promise Keeper. Perseverance in godliness does yield godly results. The church—that is, the family of God—will spend eternity rejoicing because of what the Lord God has done.

BIBLE BACKGROUND
The book of Revelation in the tradition of many books of the New Testament was written in the form of an epistle. The word "revelation" comes from the Greek word *apokalypis,* which means "a revealing or unveiling." John, a prisoner at the Roman penal colony on the Isle of Patmos in the Aegean Sea, about 30 miles off the western coast of modern Turkey, receives in a vision from God—a message for persecuted Christians. The

vision reveals God's knowledge of the church's terrible plight, how the church is responding, and God's eventual judgment and deliverance of its people. Revelation is written to encourage the Christian community to endure these hard times and continue living a life of faithfulness, love, and obedience to God.

SCRIPTURE EXPLORATION

Revelation 21:1–2—1 And I saw a new heaven and a new earth: for the first heaven and the first earth were passed away; and there was no more sea. 2 And I John saw the holy city, new Jerusalem, coming down from God out of heaven, prepared as a bride adorned for her husband.

John sees this new creation in a glorious vision and it is a welcome sight. The recreation and cleansing of both the presently devastated earthly and polluted heavenly realm above the earth is enough to shout about. This act of God is a long-awaited and expected fulfillment of a promise made by God centuries before, during the time of Isaiah (65:17; 66:22). Also seen in John's vision is a new spiritual reality coming into existence, as human beings of body and spirit are recreated with a new life in a new body. In Scripture, water is often interpreted as the symbol for people and the sea is representative of unregenerated people. The fact that there is "no more sea" reveals that the new heaven and earth only contain those who have been regenerated. Both are symbolized by the Holy City or the holy people of God coming to live in the new earth. The imagery of a bride beautifully attired, flowing with great expectation of a new and wonderful life of love with an awaiting husband, is used to depict the relationship of the people of God and their new earthly habitat.

Revelation 21:3-4—And I heard a great voice out of heaven saying, Behold, the tabernacle of God is with men, and he will dwell with them, and they shall be his people, and God himself shall be with them, and be their God. 4 And God shall wipe away all tears from their eyes; and there shall be no more death, neither sorrow, nor crying, neither shall there be any more pain: for the former things are passed away.

If the striking impact of the vision is not enough, John is further impacted by the sound of a great voice whose words he hears clearly. It's moving day. God is relocating His dwelling place from heaven to earth to live directly with His people. God's people will no longer have any sense of estrangement from Him. The mighty presence of God will bring an end to all conditions that result in human suffering and unhappiness. The sound of such heavenly words should strike a chord of resounding joy in every hearer and believer.

Revelation 21:5–7—And he that sat upon the throne said, Behold, I make all things new. And he said unto me, Write: for these words are true and faithful. 6 And he said unto me, It is done. I am Alpha and Omega, the beginning and the end. I will give unto him that is athirst of the fountain of the water of life freely. 7 He that overcometh shall inherit all things; and I will be his God, and he shall be my son.

John is directed to write down what he sees and hears, for this is not for him alone. It is a vision and message for every soul of his time and for times to come. This joy is not just for him. God's blessings are personal and communal. New lives make for new families, new neighborhoods, new cities, new nations, and ultimately, a new world. The presence of God among His people will flow freely to everyone on earth as living water, for those who drink this water are restored to wholeness and oneness with God. Everything that God has, they have—including God's name—once they have become God's child.

> *Revelation 22:3–5—And there shall be no more curse: but the throne of God and of the Lamb shall be in it; and his servants shall serve him: 4 And they shall see his face; and his name shall be in their foreheads. 5 And there shall be no night there; and they need no candle, neither light of the sun; for the Lord God giveth them light: and they shall reign for ever and ever.*

The curse of sin will depart from the earth and from the heart of humanity. In its place will be the power of God symbolized by His throne and His Lamb: Jesus. Around this core spiritual power will gather God's people for true service to Him, which is our worship. Jesus said that only the pure of heart will see God. That's why John saw God in the opening verse of this chapter. He was shown "a pure river of water of life"—the people of God. In the ancient world, the forehead is considered the seat of human consciousness. God's name there symbolizes His dominion over human consciousness. God is now the light of human understanding and wisdom, and thus victory in every realm and condition. The psalmist would say such knowledge is "too wonderful for me" (Psalm 139:6). Yet John leaves this message to be declared to every generation.

DISCUSSION

1. Using your best imaginative ability, can you envision a new earth void of all suffering? If so, share with others

your vision of this new earth. Include how you envision yourself individually and in relationship with others. Also include how you envision your family interacting with other families in community.

2. What emotions do you feel when you envision God's promise being fulfilled in the new earth?

3. Have you ever heard the voice of God speaking to you? If so, describe its effect on you at the time and what you did afterwards in response.

4. In John's vision of a new creation, what opportunities do you see for evangelism and outreach as "living water"?

5. Do you believe God's name is being written into your consciousness now? Has God's name already been written into your consciousness, or is this something that shall be written into it later? How much is God in control of you?

6. How do you recognize the church in the context of a family? Because of the goodness of God, how do you rejoice with fellow Christians?

PRACTICAL APPLICATION
PERSONAL APPLICATION

1. The birth of a child is usually met with great fanfare and celebration. Write down some of the thoughts and emotions you have as you think of such an event.

2. One of the great days of our lives is our wedding day. It is a day usually filled with great love, hope, and the expectation of living "happily ever after." Share the joy of a wedding day full of love, hope, and the expectation that the relationship will last forever with fellow class members. Use your own wedding day experience or that of someone close to you as an example.

COMMUNITY APPLICATION

1. A strong, faithful witness of the Christian message of hope and deliverance, as seen in John's vision, can have a significant impact on the lives of those yearning for a better and brighter day. If your church does not have an organized social action ministry that involves the church in the political and economic life of the community, initiate one. Begin by discussing this with church leaders and members using John's vision as the reason for the church's involvement. Attend a community association meeting to increase awareness of specific community needs and to discuss how such a ministry could become "a river of living water" to the community. Prepare for the rejoicing that will follow as lives are changed and a community is transformed.

2. Many families have an abundance of things that are unused or underused but are still in good working condition. Some things may still have their original sales tag on them! As a family or with friends, go through your house, thanking God for His goodness in giving you His blessings. Afterwards, go through the house again and with prayer, seek God's guidance to what items could be given in love, and perhaps sacrificially, to another family in need. Contact local community social service providers who may be able to share the names of distressed families or receive the items for distribution. Upon completion of this mission, return home and engage in family time of praise and worship for God's goodness, both in the receiving and the giving aspect of love.

MEDITATION

The goodness of God is anchored in the trustworthiness of

God. God is good and His goodness endures forever. God's promises of provision and deliverance are as certain as God. That is good to know because hope anchored in such knowledge becomes a sure hope. God's Word is a sure hope. To have God's Word in ones' possession—either the spoken Word or the written Word—is a great blessing. Those with eyes that see and ears that hear will have a revelation of understanding of the good news offered and fulfilled by God. Receiving and embracing this allows the Word to have dominion in your life and to transform your life into part of that refreshing river of living water. Your life can become the transforming power from the transformation of your family. Your family can become the transforming power of your community. Transformed communities can become bodies of living water for other communities to drink. The river becomes a place of refreshment and rejoicing, as change makes for a new creation filled with new life and new beginnings. Hallelujah for the passing of the old! Praise the Lord for the coming of the new!

PRAYER

Lord, our families say thank You for Your goodness and longsuffering toward us. Thank You for looking beyond our collective faults and seeing our collective needs, and for handling us with tender hands of love. With great joy we lift our collective hearts and hands to You so You may use us in the work of recreation and the ongoing fulfillment of Your promise. Yes, Lord, thy kingdom come, thy will be done here on earth as it is in heaven. Amen!

BIBLIOGRAPHY

Buttrick, George Arthur, *The Interpreter's Dictionary of the Bible*. Nashville, TN: Abingdon Press, 1982. E-J (2-3, .551-552), R-Z (100, 806-810)

Gregg, Steve._Editor. *Revelation Four Views*. A *Parallel Commentary*. Nashville, TN: Thomas Nelson Publishers, 1997.

Matthew Henry and Thomas Scott. *Matthew Henry's Concise Commentary*. Oak Harbor, WA: Logos Research Systems, 1997.

The Learning Bible Contemporary English Version. New York, NY: American Bible Society, 1995. p. 2308.

Unjhem, Arne. *The Book Of Revelation*. Philadelphia, PA: Lutheran Church Press, 1967.

NOTES

NOTES

NOTES